Recipes for Life

Food for the Body

and

Nourishment for the Soul

Compiled by Cathy Horvath

First Edition Printed, 2011

Published by: BookLogix Publishing Services, www.BookLogix.com

Editing by: Tim Morrison

Cover Art and Layout Design by: Vanessa Lowry

This book may be purchased in bulk for educational, business, fundraising or sales promotional use. For information please contact:
RecipesforLifeBodyandSoul@gmail.com
www.RecipesforLifeBodyandSoul.com

This book is compiled of stories and recipes from many contributors. Each recipe has been checked by the individual contributor. Accuracy of the recipe is solely the responsibility of the contributor. Any errors or omissions are not the responsibility of the author, compiler, editor, publisher or designer.

ISBN: 978-1-61005-058-6

Library of Congress Control Number: 2011909456

Printed in the United States of America

ACKNOWLEDGMENT

I have been referring to this "project" as my book; when indeed it has been the result of many people who have willingly and lovingly responded to my request for contributions. Several folks even came through with more than one. To each and every one of you, I extend a heartfelt "Thank You."

I thought I had a pretty good command of the English language until my editor, Tim Morrison, did what he does best—coaching a first time writer. What I thought made sense to me, many times did not make sense to him. He would question, comment, and encourage further research. I didn't like that! But in the end, I had to admit he was nearly always right! Thank you, my friend, for your guidance and expertise. I hope to do you proud.

Then there's my techno-savvy daughter Jennifer whose patience, expertise, and willingness to quickly respond to her mother's desperate plea to "straighten out this mess!" will not be forgotten. You are a treasure, my dear one, and a blessing to us all.

Thanks to Tim for introducing me to Vanessa Lowry. As the cover design artist and layout creator, she has taken my typed pages and my vision for the cover and created the lovely book before you. Vanessa, you are one of the most loving and creative people I know. I am grateful that you are in my life.

I must not forget to extend my gratitude also to Ahmad Meradji of BookLogix for his inspiration and willingness to work with a beginner writer whose grandiose ideas went far beyond what he considered a reasonable budget. I thank you and my husband thanks you—a lot!

Last, but certainly not least: Ray, my dear husband, I will be forever grateful to you for your belief in me, your support, and encouragement. You haven't changed in fifty-one years!

TABLE OF CONTENTS

TABLE OF CONTENTS

TABLE OF CONTENTS

INTRODUCTION

I had been planning to put my memories down on paper so that the younger generation of our family might have a glimpse into what took place in my life to mold me into who and what I am today. It was meant to be just a series of memories that reflect all the life lessons and experiences that I've lived through—a lot that were good, and some that were not. The elder members of my family have all passed away now, and it saddens me to realize how little information I had recorded of their lives.

Over lunch with my friend Carol Dallas, I spoke about my new project and shared that I had been thinking about including family recipes as well as life lessons. She pointed out that there was a book waiting to happen, and also declared that the title was obvious. And so this book was born. Along with the experiences that proved to be life lessons, are memories of wonderful people and the recipes for food that are tied to those memories. As I look back, I realize that among those memories are lessons that have shaped my life. I believe there are no accidents in life—only lessons and synchronistic events that are meant to guide us through our journey on this earth. In sorting through material for the book, it occurred to me that life lessons are food for the soul just as family recipes that are handed down are food for our bodies. They are all sources of energy to sustain us and help us grow.

My personal journey has taken on a new life all its own. As I shared my progress with friends, neighbors and even strangers along the way, I met with so much support and enthusiasm that I decided to reach out to others for their stories. What you will read is a collaborative effort from over 100 people—all with life lessons and/or recipes to share. So here it is: *Recipes for Life... Food for the Body and Nourishment for the Soul.* May you be uplifted, inspired, and encouraged by its contents.

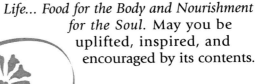

A CHILD'S VERSION OF GROWING UP

My friend, Karen, shared this remarkable story with me. From her early childhood, she never felt that she fit in—not within her own family or among her peers. She didn't feel good about herself. She never felt loved, especially by her parents. Karen attributed some of her sense of isolation to her Scandinavian background. Displays of emotions were not the norm. She felt ignored or shoved aside by her mother. "I'm just in the way . . . of everyone," she thought throughout her life. To remedy her loneliness, Karen decided to find surrogate parents who would provide the warmth and love for which she longed. Her parents knew of her search and never stood in her way. And years passed.

Back from teaching in Africa and losing a boyfriend to another Peace Corp. volunteer, Karen set forth on a spiritual journey – a journey for self-discovery. She sat amidst the Lupins (a native wildflower) on the California coast and asked that she be a channel of God. From that time on she devoted her life to following His path.

Before her mother was diagnosed with cancer, three different intuitives strongly recommended that she develop a better relationship with her mother before her mother passed on. Receiving the same advice from each one motivated her to heed their advice. As Karen visited her parents with more frequency, she was surprised to learn that they had felt unloved and ignored by her! She had thought that SHE was not wanted. The lack of open communication had caused a breach in what could have been a happy childhood and certainly a healthier family relationship. She learned the importance of understanding what each other had been thinking and feeling!

Karen's life lesson reminds us to step back and try to understand the whole picture. It's certainly not easy for children to approach parents with their perceptions. However, once into adulthood, doing so can make a big difference in how one's life is played out. Reevaluating and discussing childhood memories with the understanding of an adult can change our belief system about ourselves. That can impact our own love life, our relationship with our own children, and all those who come into our lives as lovers, friends and extended family.

A DAUGHTER'S LOVING MEMORY OF DAD

My friend, Connie Siewert, has always maintained a sense of humor and a positive attitude. When she shared this story with me, I understood where she got that from.

Connie Siewert

"My dad had recently been released from the hospital as he continued to recover from a very serious bout of pneumonia. My sister Vicki watched over Mom while Dad was hospitalized. Now that he was home, Vicki had to return to work. "It's your turn now," she said at the start of a telephone conversation. What she didn't tell me, was that he was on oxygen and that I had to drive with an oxygen tank in the car when we went for the follow-up appointment with Dad's doctor. My sister and I both have an extreme aversion to dealing with any kind of gas stored in a tank. We both laughed when my sister shared that she hadn't told me before I arrived because she was concerned that I'd refuse to come.

A few days later, after returning from the doctor's office with Dad and the tank in tow, I let out a huge sigh of relief. Once home, Dad announced he would really like chicken chow mein to celebrate his return home. He said there was a can of chicken chow mein in the pantry. I could never understand the allure of canned chow mein, but it was something that he liked and I was happy to oblige. He settled in to bed for a rest as I warmed his dinner.

Just as I was about to serve it up, he called me to the bedroom with a funny look on his face and said, "I hate to tell you this, but I am not feeling very well." We talked over his symptoms and called the home healthcare nurse. She advised us to call 911 and soon the house teemed with emergency personnel.

It was a grave scene as they worked diligently to stave off a massive heart attack. Eventually they emerged with Dad on a stretcher perched in an elevated position and hooked-up to an IV. His hair was disheveled, flopping over the oxygen tubing. He resembled one of Red Skeleton's comic characters. As they wheeled him out the door, he managed to shout the instructions "Save my chicken chow mien. I'll be back!!"

I giggled at his command while I fought back tears. Mom and I followed the ambulance to the hospital and met with the cardiologist in the Emergency Dept. He explained that Dad's heart was severely blocked. The doctor needed some more time to determine whether angioplasty surgery and implanting stents was the proper treatment or should open heart surgery be performed. He cautioned that given Dad's age and failing health, all concerned should think long and hard before making the decision. The next day we were informed that Dad was scheduled for the angioplasty and stent insertion that afternoon. In the prep room, Dad insisted on reviewing his favorite recipe for choke cherry jelly with me and made me promise to make up the batch of juice in the fridge. He always kept a supply of his homemade jelly as his special currency for good deeds and friendship gifts. He came through his surgery with flying colors and actually tickled the young cardiologist with how well it went. Pinching my dad's cheek the doctor exclaimed, "You did well Grandpa!" Dad continued his good humor in recovery telling jokes in post op to family and the hospital staff.

The stent surgery lasted quite a few years; later he was given a pacemaker. Now at 88 and his third year in a nursing home after suffering a stroke, Dad maintains his good humor. He always shares how good he feels, how he is gaining strength from physical therapy and how surprised he is that he has lived this long.

My life lesson is what a blessing it is to maintain humor in the face of a crisis. What comes to my mind as I recall the moments of life and death situations with Dad is not the sad and scary parts, but the funny moments that made me laugh. So too I recall the joy of life he still exudes even though he is not able to be mobile on his own anymore. The power of humor and positive thinking is never to be underestimated. It is such a gift to your loved ones.

Editor's note: Connie's dad passed away a few years after this experience was shared with me. Connie's visits home were more frequent and lengthy. She is a devoted daughter and oversaw her dad's care to the end.

A GOD WINK

Tricia Molloy, speaker, mentor, and author of *Divine Wisdom at Work: 10 Universal Principles for Enlightened Entrepreneurs,*

Tricia Molloy

has contributed the following lesson:

There's a lovely little book called *"When God Winks"* and in it the author writes that if you were God and you wanted to communicate with humans without using a human voice, how would you do it? You'd create coincidences, synchronicities that would prompt people to say, "What are the chances of that happening?" Those are called God Winks. My favorite God Wink happened in August of 2005 when I was putting the finishing touches on my book, *"Divine Wisdom at Work."* I was taking a long, brisk walk along the beach near my family beach home in Gulf Shores, Alabama. I started to wonder and then worry whether my book would be well received. For the longest time, this had been a personal venture and now I was about to release it to the public. I am both the author and the publisher, so I wear all the hats and I write all the checks. As I started to feel fear about money, I immediately stopped dead in my tracks, looked down at my feet and found the most perfect, tiny sand dollar. Now, you have to understand, we comb this beach every day and we have never ever found a sand dollar before. I knew in an instant that this was a God Wink. I carefully wrapped up the sand dollar and brought it home with me, placed it in a frame and keep it on my credenza in my office. Any time I feel any fear around my book or my new business of presenting Working with Wisdom talks and workshops I take a deep breath and look at that sand dollar. God winked at me and said you are successful, you are prosperous. So, whenever you are at a crossroads, in fear or trying to make a decision, start looking for those God Winks. They're all around you.

EDITOR'S NOTE: visit her web site at www.triciamolloy.com. It will inspire you.

4

A LESSON FROM THE CONVENT

Toni Thomas

There have been many lessons that have come in a variety of ways: through circumstance, friends, and of course, family and loved ones. Animals have also taught me lessons as I have observed them and experienced the joy of their company. But, if I were to choose just one it would be the lesson of just simply giving without keeping score. Or, better put – not expecting something back. So many people want to know "What's in it for me!" Such people seldom give anything of themselves unless they have a guarantee that they will be safe or get equal or more back for what they put forth. We miss out on so much of life when we do this.

When I was 19 years old I went into a Franciscan Convent in Syracuse, NY. I wanted to be a nun and live my life that way. I researched my elementary school nuns, contacted the Mother Superior and entered the Franciscan Convent on September 8, 1968.

Convent life was very interesting and enlightening. I stayed only six months, but long enough to know that I wouldn't stay there forever. In fact, the day I entered the convent I knew I would someday leave.

While there I met some fascinating women. One was Sister Ann Michael, the Novice Directress (or Mistress as we called her then). During one of her lectures she told us that as long as we were in the convent we were going to "give and give and give until we had nothing left to give. Then we were going to give some more." This brings me to my life lesson about giving. Her words still ring in my head now as she said them almost 40 years ago: "Give until you have nothing left to give ..." Whether it's money, food from the pantry, or your services, we all have something to give unto others. That's important to remember in all of our dealings with people. Most of us think of what we will get back even before we begin the process of giving. (Is this going to be a tax deduction, is it really needed, let the government do something about it, etc.) In doing so, we miss the true joy of the moment which can never be measured in dollars or material goods.

So, my most important life lesson learned many years ago is still with me today and has served me well spiritually, emotionally and every way possible.

EDITOR'S NOTE: This lesson was written by a dear friend of mine who is a nationally recognized astrologer. I can attest to the fact that she lives what she writes. She is a most kind and generous person, always looking out for ways to help others. I don't think an unkind or nasty word has ever left her mouth. What an example for us all!

A LIGHT BULB AT AGE 36

One of my closest friends is a successful psychotherapist and is well known for her specialty, sandtray therapy, as well as her collaboration with an equine specialist in the Atlanta area to do equine assisted psychotherapy. Here is her life lesson:

"Growing up, I was the shy, quiet one. I was a first born, and the traditional high achiever, in spite of my stay-in-the-background ways. My sister was the bubbly, cute one who never knew a stranger. My father died when I was 4 years old and my mother, sister and I lived with my grandparents. My memories are mostly that Mom, only 18 years older than I, worked and dated. My grandmother was into community service. My sister and I were taken along wherever she went and given tasks as appropriate. My grandfather was quiet and erudite. I used to enjoy the occasional attention from him when he invited me to do crossword puzzles with him. He needed no help, but I felt special. Birthdays were celebrated and the whole family gathered on special occasions, which were frequently held at our house. We played sports, attended Sunday school and belonged to groups. What I learned from my family was to stay out of trouble; do my best, etc. My physical needs were met, but there was little emotional connection. To me, childhood felt pretty normal and was relatively uneventful.

I went to college because it followed high school. Many girls my age continued their schooling to find a husband. I didn't think that would happen, so I wanted an education to fall back on. Although I felt myself to be okay, I never dated a lot and figured I would probably never marry. I tried not to think about it; just complete my education so I could support myself.

I was so surprised when I fell in love with a handsome, very intelligent young man with a lot of ambition. As was common in the day, we were "equals", yet I always went with his choices because I wanted him to be happy.

I was totally unaware of the effects that child abuse could have on one's adult life. I thought my husband had "risen above" the trauma of his family. Because he paid attention to me, I felt loved. I did not understand his burden of being the eldest child and having to protect his younger siblings from two abusive alcoholic parents as much as possible. His childhood experiences meant that my husband, too, did not learn to "connect". It would not be until my 40s that I would understand the long term affects. He became a dentist. When he finished his residency, we settled just outside Atlanta.

After 7 1/2 years of marriage and infertility problems, we adopted a baby girl. Five months later, I surprisingly got pregnant and gave birth to a baby boy who arrived almost two months early. We were lucky our son had only minor medical issues. I remember clearly being reminded to make sure I did not ignore my husband just because I had two babies to care for. I thought I was doing a good job. When the children were 1 and 2 years old, we moved to a larger house. I thought I became good at entertaining and keeping the social calendar, as well as taking care of my husband and the children. I minimized the growing issues of unrest in my marriage. Life's timing was overwhelming for my husband. Every year in November, we had a major event – new practice, new house, adopted newborn baby, another newborn. I thought life was good. Actually, the problems we had managed to sweep under the carpet before children were no longer so easy to sweep away. He became more demanding and critical of me. I wore rose-colored glasses and blinders to anything my husband did that should have not been tolerated. I did not stand up for myself nor confront any issues. I did not understand what was happening, nor did I know how my own neediness contributed to our problems. I loved him and was proud he was so successful, but I began to question what I thought was love.

Although I didn't often have time to read, someone had recommended that I purchase a fictional book, *The Women's Room*, and make time to read it. Mia, the main character, seemed to speak to me. The story was about a young couple who were so much in love. He was a medical student. After 16 or more years of marriage and two children, her husband comes home and announces that he wants a divorce. Mia is surprised and devastated. She had not realized he had been unhappy. What will happen to her? The story continues about how she gets back on her feet, raises her children and returns to school, eventually "finding" herself. It seemed to me that the message of the book was, "There ain't nobody there but you, Babe!" Meaning, parents die, children grow up and move away, and a significant other may or may not stay around. I think that Mia was unaware. This mirrored my life and my fears of being alone and unconnected. I coped by minimizing our issues and didn't realize how my lack of life skills had not helped our marriage. I had thought that I was doing everything I could to be everything my husband wanted.

Problems at home escalated. Counseling for us, both separately and together, was of little help. I believe that the book subconsciously triggered me and I awoke one morning, feeling as though I had been in a fog for 36 years. How had I functioned? A light bulb went off as I realized I had to do something/everything differently. It truly felt like this was the first day of the rest of my life!

When I filed for divorce, it was not because I did not love my husband. It was because I could no longer stay with him. I had become physically afraid of him. It felt as if he was having a nervous breakdown and there was nothing I could do. Even the psychologist did not diagnose his depression much less any other issues. My presence seemed to only make matters worse. We eventually divorced.

With help from a career counselor, I went to graduate school and became a psychotherapist, specializing in child abuse and dysfunctional families. I now understand so much more about what happened in my life, including what our therapists did not recognize. Through therapy, I learned to be stronger, to communicate better; I became able to assertively confront. In other words, I found my voice.

I successfully raised two beautiful children who now have children of their own, and I am finding myself. It has been a journey, a process. It has not been easy, but it has been worth every struggle. I still have bumps in the road and find that, although I may stumble, I can get up and go on. My experiences have helped me to be more successful in my occupation as well as in life. I am adding new people and things in my world. Life is beautiful!"

A WILL TO LIVE

Originally published in the March 2011 issue of CountyLine magazine.
Permission to reprint by Sugarcane Communications, LLC, the publisher of CountyLine.

Love, hope, and a will to live! Every parent strives hard to instill these three very important ingredients into the minds and hearts of their children. In October of last year, our family suffered the most tragic loss imaginable, the death of our son, Richard Williams "Will" Trautwein. At 15-years-old, Will was unable to see the love and hope that surrounded him, and his will to live disappeared. Whether it disappeared for a long time, or for a moment, does not matter, the fact is that it disappeared, and a family and a community were left to pick up the "light" that once shown so brightly in Will.

John Trautwein

Since that dreadful day in October, we have survived one day at a time, carried by our faith, our family and a complete submersion in love from our friends that has been nothing short of miraculous.

As a result, the Will to Live Foundation, Inc. was formed. Our mission, quite simply is: *"To create a non-profit foundation that is dedicated to improving the lives and the 'Will to Live' of teenagers everywhere. Through education, motivation, consultation, charity, support and most importantly, love and fellowship, we will work for and through these young adults to help them always find the 'Good' in life and a 'Will to live' through all of life's trials."*

Will Trautwein was a young man who truly loved his friends. A "win" for Will was friendship. We have learned from his friends that he never had a bad thing to say about anyone, and he embraced everyone for exactly who they were. He loved them, and he made sure they knew it. His family takes comfort in knowing that if he were here today, he would be demanding a leading role in this foundation, and this gives us strength.

THE CLARENCE EFFECT

The first event for the foundation was in December of 2010. The girl's lacrosse team at Northview High School organized a charity fundraiser showing of *It's a Wonderful Life*. At a Fellowship of Christian Athletes meeting just four weeks before, I was asked to speak to a small section of the Northview High student body. With my wife at my side, we delivered a message that was simple: "Love each other, be there for each other, but most importantly, talk to each other. Help each other find the good in life!" We introduced "The Clarence Effect" by challenging the kids to be more like Clarence in *It's a Wonderful Life*—that friend who helps another find the good in life, even at the worst of times. "Who's your Clarence?" we asked. "This holiday tell them!"

After the viewing of this classic movie, the Facebook posts and the emails and "Clarence" references were everywhere. We so much enjoyed watching and listening to these high school students talking about Clarence and being that "guardian angel" for each other and realizing that we all need a Clarence or two— "Life Teammates" to help find the good in life's difficult times.

MY LIFE TEAMMATES

"The human spirit craves companionship." A good friend and life teammate of mine, Brian Holman (ex-Major league pitcher) said this to me not long after my son passed. He wanted to make sure I was seeking companionship to help me through this most difficult time. Brian embodies the perfect definition of what we at the foundation term a "Life Teammate." A friend who I shared a dream with, along with joy, success and failures almost 25 years ago (when I was one of these young adults). Yet now, Brian is still there for me, and he was letting me know it—and he is one of many.

My wife Susie and I were both athletes for so much of our lives and have always been part of a team in one way, shape or form. We developed such strong bonds with these friends who we now consider "Life Teammates." Our children are developing these bonds now, and with the pressures on young adults in today's world, they are needed more than ever before.

H.E. Luccock once said: "No one can whistle a symphony. It takes an orchestra to play it." Well, the Will to Live Foundation believes that "Life is a Symphony" and it sounds so much better when you share it with friends whom you love!

My six-year-old daughter Holyn recently drew for me a lovely picture of her "Life Teammates"—those people in her life that she would want to help and those people she would turn to for help. Later that night at dinner, she and her brothers discussed the drawing, and it was a wonderful moment. We then asked, "Do they know they are your 'Life Teammates?'"—Holyn could not answer. "Wouldn't they feel wonderful, Holyn, knowing that you considered them a 'Life Teammate?'"

RAISING AWARENESS

The foundation is not about raising money. Yes, we will raise money so we can make donations to help finance the suicide prevention and counseling experts in our communities. We want to fund teen suicide awareness events, and we want to fund various scholarships to young adults as well. But the true goal is to help create a stronger "Will to Live" in our teen communities.

In February, in a small town in New Hampshire, a 13-year-old girl named Emma, who discovered the "Will To Live Group" on Facebook, created a "Teen Suicide Awareness" month at her middle school in North Andover MA. They are giving motivational music CDs for donations, selling Will to Live bracelets, holding bake sales, and giving away teen suicide awareness pamphlets. They may raise $200, but more importantly, the kids of that community will have worked together forming life bonds while educating themselves, their classmates, and their community of the teen suicide epidemic and the need for all of us to work together to create that life symphony—that "Will to Live."

For more information on the Will to Live Foundation, visit: www.will-to-live.org. You may contact both John and Susie Trautwein at: friends@will-to-live.org.

ALL ARE DIVINE CREATIONS

Several years ago, I was introduced to a little book entitled *Angelspeake* by authors Trudy Griswold and Barbara Mark. It's an easy read and most importantly, an easy guide on how to communicate with your Guardian Angels.

Cathy Horvath

Angelspeake is a step by step primer on connecting and receiving loving responses. I want to share a very moving response I received while flying from Chicago to a management meeting in Irvine, CA. I usually sit in an aisle seat close to the bulkhead (I'm claustrophobic). But this time I followed an associate's advice and requested a window seat. Paul said the view was too spectacular to miss by sitting in the aisle. I spent the first half of the trip working on my laptop, fine tuning my presentation for the meeting, and going over my notes. When I decided to shut down and take a look out the window, I was in awe of the views. From what I could figure out, the plane was flying over the Central Plains of Iowa and Nebraska, parts of Colorado, Utah and then continued over the North rim of the Grand Canyon. The flight proceeded to its destination in the southern part of California. The farmlands of the Central Plains looked like perfect patchwork quilts in soft shades of green and tan. The mountains of Colorado and Utah were magnificent and the Grand Canyon an awesome, majestic site.

"How could anyone not believe in God, or a divine source of Creation, when they observe these sights?" I thought to myself. I pulled out a pad of paper and wrote to my Angels. I couldn't think of what to say or what to ask, so as I sometimes do, I simply invited them to share a message with me. This is their response. It is one I have shared with many people.

"As you look out the airplane window and are awed by the beauty of the Divine creation of the rivers, lakes, forests, and mountains, know that each and every one of you is just as magnificent a Divine creation. Yes, indeed, you are each that special and beautiful, yet you fail to appreciate your magnificence. That is an affront to the Creator. It's like telling God that the majestic mountains and the Grand Canyon are no big deal! Isn't that awful? And yet that's what little value you place on yourself and others; what little appreciation you have for the magnificence that is you! Just as every earthly creature has been planned for and is cared for, so too is each and every one of your brothers and sisters on earth. Outward appearances are deceiving because inside every human being is a spiritual being that has been planned for and is being watched over regardless of their words and deeds. Please keep this reminder tucked in your heart the next time you have the urge to judge another. Know that each one is playing out a role and needs your love to further them along. Unconditional love is an energy. It is like no other that generates tremendous spiritual growth for the sender and for the receiver as well. Unconditional love, act by act, step by step, brings you one step closer to connecting with your divinity. We will leave you with these thoughts for now. Our love is with you always."

AMY'S HAM BBQ

Amy Morton was my personal trainer here in the Atlanta area. I met her when I decided to stop being a couch potato and start taking good care of my body. Having never engaged in formal physical activity in my life, I was quite apprehensive. I enjoy brisk walking and biking, but this was something else altogether. Amy changed all that, however, and I actually looked forward to our sessions each week. Her approach is specific to age, lifestyle, physical condition and each person's goal. There is no "cookie cutter" program in her repertoire. As an explanation for her contribution to this book, she writes: "Here is my Grandma's Ham BBQ recipe. It is a big hit with my family. It is a quick meal that my Mom whips up in no time. The idea of a Ham BBQ is pretty unique to Pittsburgh, PA." (That's Amy's hometown.)

Amy Morton

AMY'S
HAM
BBQ

INGREDIENTS

1 small bottle of ketchup (HEINZ, of course!)

1/2 cup water

1 tablespoon brown sugar

1 tablespoon strawberry jam/jelly

1 tablespoon vinegar

1 teaspoon mustard

1 dash of salt

1/4 cup diced onions (if desired)

1 lb. chipped deli ham

PREPARATION

Put first 8 ingredients in a pot on the stovetop. Cook on low heat for 1/2 hour. Add 1 lb of chipped (thinly sliced) ham. Cook for another 15-20 minutes over low heat.

Serve on a hearty bun.

AN EQUESTRIAN LESSON

Alison Kelly authors a monthly newsletter on her web site. www.KnowingAngels.com.

Alison Kelly

I look forward to her inspirational messages and stories that are uplifting and brighten my day. One such personal story captured my heart. An avid equestrian, she opened by saying that a recent "adoption", Mr. Forrest, is more than just a horse to her daughter and herself. With her permission I will share her lesson with you.

"Mr. Forrest is a Bay Quarter horse and was bred for competition in the rodeo arena. His former owners had high expectations and worked him tirelessly. When he was no longer able to perform to their standards, they donated him to a non-profit group that worked with developmentally challenged children. Unfortunately, he had developed a bad attitude and did not easily conform to the program. He would refuse to move forward when the kids were attempting to ride him. He was quite stubborn and of course, of no use to the program. After being passed around from barn to barn, he ended up being labeled a liability that couldn't be trained. He was left in an open field without proper shelter or adequate food. There he lived for many years.

My daughter Jade loves horses. She struggles with severe learning disabilities and processing issues. Unfortunately, she is a very intuitive nine year old girl who understood that she was different from other kids her age. She was unable to attend public school and placed in a special school that could help with her struggles. This took a toll on her self-esteem and compounded her challenges. It wasn't until I witnessed her special bond with horses and the self-confidence she held when riding, that I realized the potential of that bond.

We found Mr. Forrest on a windy cold day standing in an open field. He was shy and mistrustful; but we could see something magical in his eyes. The next day, we moved him into a beautiful 30 acre farm that was within walking distance from our house. Jade spent countless hours grooming him, talking to him, and just walking around the property with him. It has been three years and the two of them have become "soul-mates". Just yesterday, with great confidence, they were racing across the fields at a full canter, both with big smiles! The horse that everyone rejected and said could never be ridden, knows he carries precious cargo on his back. He loves her and she loves him. They have taught each other how to have strength, power, and ability to rise above it all...and I have learned that a little love can go a long way!

AN EXTRAORDINARY MOTHER'S RECIPE

"My late mother was an extraordinary woman. She entered our country when she was only 13 years old to escape the events happening in her native Germany.

Carole Tomlinson, Author

Helma Hornung was engaged to a handsome blonde haired blue eyed young man named Hans. He joined the Hitler Youth Program and eventually became an officer in the dreaded SS Nazi organization. She would have no part of this and left Germany to make a life in New York City. She had lost her mother when she was four years old and was raised by a loving Grandmother. Helma taught herself English by reading street signs and conversing with many people. One day she was discovered by a modeling agency. She became a hat model and encountered a Hollywood agent. Helma was asked to audition for a major movie studio. Exactly at that time she met my father and instead decided to devote herself to having children and being a good wife. She was a beautiful woman and attracted many people who adored her. I will always remember her doing volunteer work to help others. My mother was a giver and helped organize a literacy program which involved sending books out to children in underdeveloped countries. She always instructed my brother and me to learn one new word daily as she did.

My mother was a wonderful cook and made many loaves of this delicious banana bread which she always distributed to sick people and our neighbors. Her credo was: 'Never be sharp. Never be flat. Always be natural.' That is how she taught me to just be myself."

HELMA'S BANANA BREAD RECIPE ON THE NEXT PAGE

HELMA'S BANANA BREAD

INGREDIENTS

2 mashed bananas

1/4 pound butter

1/4 cup granulated sugar

2 eggs

1 teaspoon lemon juice

2 cups sifted flour

3 teaspoons baking powder

1/4 teaspoons salt

1/2 cup raisins

1/2 cup chopped nuts

PREPARATION:

Cream shortening and sugar together.

Beat eggs until light and add.

Press bananas through sieve or mash. Add lemon juice. Blend with creamed mixture.

Sift flour, baking powder and salt together and mix quickly into banana mixture. Add nuts and raisins.

Bake in greased bread loaf pan at 350 degrees about 1 hour. Makes 1 lb. loaf.

ANGEL LOVE, IT'S UNCONDITIONAL

Cathy Horvath

No, it's not part of a song. Rather, it was a response from my Guardian Angels several years ago when I was in a particularly sad place emotionally. I lamented that I had been through so many tough times with relationships that it was difficult for me to fathom someone or something genuinely loving me for just me—unconditionally. I actually told my angels that we humans are conditioned to believe that there is something about us that is not loveable and that is reinforced every day by someone, somehow. It is hard to accept that my Guardian Angels and all God's angels love me no matter what. What follows is their response.

"We understand where you are coming from and we are trying hard to fix that perception. God is all about loving uncon- ditionally, and we are an expression of God. So we are a part of that unconditional love. If everyone knew that they could rely on our unconditional love for reinforcement of the good person that they are, there would be less hatred and violence and overall unkindness in your world. People would not have to stoop to unkind or violent measures towards others to make themselves feel superior or good about themselves. If their parents have not showered them with love whether they behaved properly or not, if their teachers were unkind, prejudiced, if their friends gave them a hard time or judged them harshly, if their boss gave them a rough time and made them feel inferior—so what? This is man's evaluation from his perspective—not God's. You see, no matter what is happening on the physical plane, God is always present with His unconditional love pouring out to you and others. Trouble is, you don't know how to accept it and you don't truly believe that it's possible because you have been conditioned otherwise. This is the time for new beginnings as you live in a new millennium. Why not alter your point of view? The old way hasn't worked too well; why not give this a shot as they say? What if, God made you feel good about yourself even if your mother or father doesn't—would that make you feel better? What if, the cruelty your brother or sister displays towards you could be offset and weakened by the fact that they don't matter as much as God's viewpoint and affection for you does? What if, the cruelty that pervades the corporate world would not impact you any longer because you know your worth in God's eyes and that's all that really matters? Would that not change your work? The surprise is that it would for you internally, but at the same time your reaction to these hurts and cruelties would also change how the world treats you because one is affected by the other. When you change internally an external change follows—that is the law of the Universe. Even if you think these thoughts quietly to yourself when an injustice or unkindness is being dealt you, somehow you will notice that the other person will perceive their efforts are not penetrating your consciousness and they are not getting the results they had expected. After a while, they will discontinue in their efforts because you are not responding as they would expect.

Love unconditionally is a tough one and yet you give it so freely to infants and pets, do you not? How is it so much harder to love another human being in the same way—think about that?"

ANGEL MESSAGE; HOW TO MAKE A DIFFERENCE

What seems to be happening is that your society is getting numb to all the happenings around the world. It is as if the wars, the poverty and the killings and beatings are just another made for television movie. True there are many, many people who are giving up their lives to help the world, but it is in the power of every one in your world, on planet earth to make a difference. And it isn't always about money. One small gesture in the home, one act of kindness in your community, one small donation to a cause has a ripple effect into the large pool that is the entire world. The images that you see in news reports and magazines are real. The people suffering are real. If they appeared at your doorstep you would jump at the chance to make a difference in their lives. Consider that the television screen is presenting someone on your doorstep. Select one issue, one cause and start there. Doing nothing won't change the world. The politicians

Cathy Horvath

won't and can't change without every human being's support.

Select one thing that the television has brought to your doorstep and take it as a personal mission to change things. You can all do that. One person at a time. Before you know it, you have an entire community making a difference. Whether it is at home, in your community, in your city, in your state, or wherever, something good will happen. The babies, mothers, fathers, and soldiers you watch on the television screen are crying out to you. "Help me, my brother. Don't let this happen to me!"

Mother Earth herself is crying out the same way. "Help me, my child; don't let this happen to me!" Don't let me be destroyed so that your children and your children's children will not know life in all it beauty as you do. And so it is for now. Our blessings to you this day and every day.

ANGELS COME IN MANY FORMS

Cathy Horvath

On a Friday afternoon in late November, 2009 I rushed my husband Ray to the Emergency Room of the new hospital just up the road from us. He had back pains all week just under his shoulder blades. No matter what sports cream or heating pad, or ice pack he tried, the pain kept getting worse. Ray seldom complains. However, as the week progressed he began complaining with more frequency. When Friday late afternoon arrived and Ray continued struggling with his pain, I got my car keys, put on my coat, handed him his jacket and said "that's it…we're heading for the hospital, okay?" I was amazed at his response when he got his coat on and said "Let's go." That's not like him so I knew his discomfort had to be severe. I dropped him off at the Emergency entrance and parked the car. When I entered the Emergency lobby a nurse led me to the room in which Ray had been placed. I entered the room and found Ray attended to by five different medical personnel. "Wow, I thought. All this for a back ache?"

Not so. He was having a massive heart attack. The new Emory Johns Creek Hospital did not have a heart unit yet. So within minutes Ray was prepared for transfer and airlifted to Emory University Hospital in Decatur, GA. The staff explained that every minute counted because he was losing heart muscle. It was dark outside as I stood on the sidewalk a few yards away from the helicopter pad and watched them take off into the night sky.

Now here's where the Angel comes in. In the 10 years I have lived in Atlanta, I have travelled mostly within the communities north of the city, close to where I live. When I have had cause to go to Decatur, I have found the layout of the town, southeast of the city, to be very confusing. Every time I have attended a social function there in daylight, I get lost. My friends joke that I need an escort every time I visit Decatur. Now I have to get there in the dark and all by myself! The nurses printed out a MapQuest for me and gave me directions as to where to go once I arrived at the hospital. One of the EMT's from the helicopter also gave me some hints and reassured me that I would be fine. The nurses asked if they could call someone to be with me, but all my grown children were in Tampa celebrating my son's birthday. One friend was out of town, the others would require too much time to catch up with me, so I headed for the road. As I approached my car, I looked up at the stars in the sky and called upon my Angels to guide me and get me there quickly. I'll admit, even though I knew they heard me and would help, I was very apprehensive about finding my way to Decatur in the dark!

Well, I almost made it. However, at one point when I exited the Interstate highways and got into town, I looked up and saw a different street name than the one I was supposed to be on. Oh brother! I turned off the road and took another look at the MapQuest. I don't know where I am! How am I supposed to follow this map when the street name isn't on here! With that my cell phone rang and it was the EMT from the helicopter. He told me that Ray was already in the operating room and doing fine. He then asked how I was doing and I told him that true to my worry, I was lost. He asked what I saw around me and when I described the buildings, he said I was very near the hospital, not to worry. He then stayed with me and proceeded to guide me through the stop lights, turn off, and streets until I reached the entrance to the hospital. He told me what elevator bank to take to the Cardiac Wing, and how to get directly to the operating room. Now I ask you, was he my Angel messenger or what?! I would say my Guardian Angels answered my plea for help. They will do the same for you; all you have to do is ask.

P.S. Ray had an angioplasty on one artery that night and a quadruple bypass the following Tuesday. He has recovered beautifully, much to the amazement of our family and friends. He returned to his part time job within six weeks of his surgeries and looks healthier than ever.

ANNE BAXTER'S CHRISTMAS GIFT

Melissa Galt

Christmas was approaching and my sisters and I were once again stymied on what to get our Mom. She had everything she could want and what she didn't have, she'd get herself. (She was Ann Baxter, star of stage and screen, with an Oscar on the mantel!) So what on earth could we give her that would be special, memorable, and desired? She asked, and finally, we listened and delivered . . . a flexible flyer. I know, it sounds crazy. Here she was at fifty-five years of wisdom but she had always wanted a wooden sled, better known in her day as a flexible flyer. She'd made the request before but we never took it seriously. At this point we finally considered that maybe she really did know what she wanted and rather than over think it, and give what we each thought would be best, we'd just fulfill the wish. So simple, yet so significant.

Come Christmas Eve, we gathered on the stone patio on our home in rural Connecticut. We were joined by a family friend, Gusty Hornblower (short for Augusta, and yes that was her real name!) Within a few minutes, Gusty disappeared to parts unknown, leaving my Mom, two sisters and me on the patio bundled in our wintery best. Here we presented Mom with the sled of her dreams. She was a fur bound creature that night. Standing a petite 5'3 (she always claimed and 3/4 inches) with her rabbit fur boots and her lynx coat to the top of those, she laughed with glee and clapped her hands in delight as she saw us pull out her new toy. She promptly dropped it off the edge of the patio and slid giggling all the way to the bottom of the hill. Suddenly Santa Claus appeared from behind a tree near Mom's landing place, and began trudging up the hill, "ho-ho-hoing" all the way hoisting a large sack on his back. Mom was startled but amused. Yes, it did turn out to be our friend Gusty, but for one brief shining moment in my adult life, I was a mere child of six again, and my Mother was her own little girl again, wrapped in warm woolies and dusted with snow from her ride down the hill.

It was a magical Eve, never seen before or since and one I will always cherish. I learned then that magic happens when you least expect it, when you can be a child again, and when you listen and deliver instead of over thinking, over analyzing, and being such a grown up. Find your inner child and you'll tap your own magic.

ANNE'S QUEEN CAKES SAVE THE DAY

The following is an excerpt from the forthcoming book, "At Home in Lissaphuca".

For much of my life I heard Irish songs telling of folks longing for the old country – to go back home to Ireland. Books and photos of the scenery, tiny remote cottages and people enjoying each others' hospitality captivated and enchanted me. When we were able to do so, my husband and I decided to go to Ireland and live much as my ancestors must have. When we visited the area where they originated, I knew that was the spot for my adventure. For nine years we lived in our own tiny cottage, while we connected with the people and the land.

Molly Alexander Darden

When we first moved into our cottage in Lissaphuca, a seven-home far-flung community in the foothills of the Slieve Aughty Mountains of Galway, Ireland, I wondered about the intricacies of entertaining on the "come anytime" basis of visiting in the Irish countryside. As usual, Anne Costello, our mentor and neighbor, showed us the ropes.

Imagine – it's the evening before your grocery shopping day; the cupboards are pretty much bare. You've finished the dinner dishes and settled in front of the TV. The doorbell rings. What in the world to give the drop-in visitors?

No panic, as Anne had told me. Just mix up a batch of Queen Cakes. You can't go wrong with them for most occasions. The kitchen of our traditional-style cottage is divided into two rooms; the front ("big kitchen") is a combination sitting/food preparation/dining room, while the back kitchen (scullery) is used for washing up and extra storage.

Well, with our set-up it isn't possible to scurry around in the kitchen without company knowing about the dilemma of nearly empty cupboards, but it doesn't matter because our on-the-spot- preparation is hardly noticed. Just keep on talking as I mix up the batter.

First, though, put on the kettle for tea or coffee (usually tea), and if the night is cold and blustery the first of our hot water might go into a hot whiskey for our guests.

Out in the country with no local daily newspapers, word-of-mouth com-munication is vital. The initial question is nearly always, "What's the news? Who's sick? Who's back from America (or leaving for it)? Who's pregnant, getting married, etc., and sadly, who's died?" It's important to keep current because for all important public occasions virtually the entire community turns out. Now, your conversation is off and running, the cakes are in the oven, and you're all settled in for a lovely evening's chat. The hours will melt away. Here is a tiny taste of that experience:"

ANNE'S QUEEN CAKE

INGREDIENTS AND PREPARATION

With this recipe you can hardly go wrong, but practice does make perfect.

Cream together some butter (margarine) and sugar, equal amounts, according to how many guests you have.

Beat up an egg (more for a large group), add a few handfuls of "self-raising" flour, mix well and add the butter, sugar and some milk to make the proper consistency of cake batter. Any favorite flavorings, if not considered too exotic by your guests, will add to the pleasure.

Mix batter well, pour into a greased pan and pop into the oven at medium temperature.

If your "cooker" burns solid fuel as ours does, you quickly learn to gauge whether to put your item on the shelf or the bottom of the oven.

After approximately seven minutes, turn your cake pan 1/2 turn, and continue baking. The lovely aroma will add to the cozy, relaxed atmosphere you've just created.

Be sure to keep the stove stoked with turf, wood or coal to keep the heat up. Seven minutes later, check your cake with a toothpick or knife for doneness, take it out, allow to cool, and if you have some, top each slice with a bit of jam or cream.

Serve with another pot of steaming tea, and settle in for the "craic." (Irish for "fun.")

ANOTHER VIEWPOINT ON VIOLENCE

We take so much for granted these days and assume we can do nothing to change the way things are that are not to our liking or for our benefit. On one subject my Guardian Angels had a different viewpoint. I have learned to communicate with my Guardian Angels several years ago. Trudy Griswold and Barbara Mark wrote a primer describing how. It is a quick read, and when I'm concerned about something, I simply sit in a quiet place, relax my body and ask my Angels for a message that is appropriate for the time. I "hear" words and phrases in my head that I know are not mine and I write them down or type them on my computer. I keep those messages and refer back to them from time to time to inspire and uplift me. Here is one such message:

Cathy Horvath

"Members of the earth family are missing the mark by indulging in superficial means of easing the pain that is all around them. Besides drugs and alcohol, they watch the news and witness violence and disrespect towards others' religious beliefs. They watch the news and see murders and acts of violence enacted upon others. They watch television shows and follow violent war and thriller series. They attend movies and are mesmerized by violence and war atrocities, destruction of property, and killing. What is happening to this and the younger generations who witness this and consider this entertainment? It comes to pass that they soon will not know the difference between real life and entertainment. That is happening already. Why are these horrible viewings acceptable to the world's societies?

Yet you wonder why your children are becoming more and more violent in the home, in school and on the streets. They have been exposed to countless hours of this anti-Christ behavior. Anti-Christ behavior is the right term because to do harm to another is not honoring the Christ within each and every person on this earth. It is unthinkable to us that verbal or physical harm would be imposed to the body that was created by God. If God were in front of these offenders they would fall to their knees and beg forgiveness for they do know what they are doing but they do not know that it is God that they are offending.

It is incumbent upon parents, family members, teachers, ministers of all religions to impart this message to their loved ones. The message of Jesus is being lost among those who put power and greed before all else. We leave you with this. Ponder our words and pray to us for help. All you have to do is ask and we are there to help return your world to its rightful place of peace and tranquility. It is possible, not a pipedream."

ASHLEY'S PEPPERMINT CANDY

The Holidays are always a special time in the Horvath household, and Christmas 2000 was no exception. However, it was a little different from "the old days" because my husband and I had recently moved to the Atlanta area from Chicago, where we had lived all our lives.

Ashley Huber

I was most grateful when our daughters Robyn and Jennifer and granddaughters Ashley and Lauren drove seven and a half hours from Tampa to be with us. Like most kitchens at Christmastime, ours bustled with activity as we baked cookies, brownies, pizelles and whatever else we could think of to keep our two granddaughters occupied and not thinking of the huge pile of gifts awaiting them under the tree. Not to be outdone, eight year old Ashley stared at the counter of ingredients and proceeded to create the following recipe with her mom's help. I think she and her classmates made it at school before the holiday break. It is so easy and delicious that I insisted she write it down for me. Don't wait for Christmas to try it; it only has two ingredients so how hard can it be?

ASHLEY'S
PEPPERMINT
CANDY

INGREDIENTS

2 lbs Bakers white chocolate or any good quality white chocolate

30 small candy canes

PREPARATION

Line a jelly roll pan with heavy-duty tin foil. Melt the chocolate in a microwaveable bowl on medium setting for 5-6 minutes stirring occasionally until the chocolate is melted and smooth. Put the candy canes in a sturdy plastic bag or between two pieces of waxed paper. Use a rolling pin to break the candy into small chunks. Stir the candy into the melted chocolate. Spread the mixture evenly into the jelly roll pan. Chill about 45 minutes to an hour until set. Or freeze for a few minutes. Break into pieces by slamming pan on the counter, or just use your hands to break into small pieces.

AUNT LENA'S TUNA POT PIE

Cathy Horvath

Have you ever known someone who is so kind, loving and gentle that they wouldn't even kill a fly? They will take great measures to usher a mosquito, fly, spider, or any other pesky insect out the window or door before they would consider killing it. Have you ever known someone who talks to their plants and their pets like they're family? They really do consider them family members. Their plants flourish when no one else has had success in doing so. I had the privilege of having a member of the family that fits that description—my Aunt Lena.

She was a devout woman whose life centered on her home and family. I remember her serving this dish one Friday evening when my family visited her and Uncle Joe and their two children. It was so delicious that shortly after I married and began collecting my favorite recipes, I asked Aunt Lena to share it with me. Of course, she gladly complied.

AUNT LENA'S TUNA POT PIE

INGREDIENTS

1 cup water

1/2 teaspoon salt

1/2 cup diced raw carrots

1 cup diced raw potatoes

3 tablespoons chopped onion

1 cup green peas

Liquid from peas (water from frozen or juice from canned)

2 tablespoons butter

1 7oz. can flaked tuna (save oil)

2 tablespoons flour

Milk to add to vegetable liquid to make 2 cups

1/2 teaspoon salt

Dash of pepper

PREPARATION

Simmer carrots, potatoes and onion for 15 minutes in salted water. Add peas and simmer for 5 more minutes. Melt butter in saucepan and add oil from tuna. Stir in flour; liquid, salt and pepper. Cook until thickened, stirring constantly. Add drained vegetables and tuna. Turn into a 6x10x2 inch baking dish. Cover with Pastry Topping.

PASTRY TOPPING INGREDIENTS

1 cup flour

1/2 teaspoon salt

1/3 cup shortening

2 tablespoons water

Combine ingredients and roll out to a size that covers the baking dish. Allow a little extra for crimping the edges.

Bake in hot oven (450 degrees) 25 to 30 minutes or until crust is browned.

AUNT LILL'S CRESCENT COOKIES

She lived in a small, dark, damp little cottage in Downer's Grove, Illinois. She was related to us as my father's aunt, his mother's sister. Her habitat was of heavy, dark draperies and furniture. There

Bill Joch

was no soft carpeting to walk on, only wooden floors that were so warped from lack of insulation that one had to watch their step as not to fall. Her name was Lillian, known to us as Aunt Lill. She was short and plump. First thought of Aunt Lill is her bending over to give me a big juicy kiss. Never liked that part. Then we would follow her waddle to the kitchen for a snack. Looking back it seemed that every time we went there we had Aunt Lill"s crescent cookies which were full of butter, crushed pecans and powdered sugar. To this day every time I make her crescent cookies I have fond memories of Aunt Lill.

AUNT LILL'S
CRESCENT
COOKIES

INGREDIENTS

1 cup softened butter

2 cups flour

2 cups finely chopped pecans

5 tablespoons of sugar

1 tablespoon water

2 teaspoons vanilla powdered sugar

PREPARATION

Mix all ingredients together. Break off a piece of dough about the size of a walnut and form into crescents. Bake on ungreased cookie sheet at 325 degrees for 20 min. Cool for 5 minutes and roll in powdered sugar.

AUNT MARGE'S POTATO SALAD

Cathy Horvath

My mom was known for her wonderful potato salad. Folks requested that she make it for picnics and all other family gatherings. Mom couldn't take credit for it, however, because she actually got the recipe from a dear friend, Marge Dailey. We called her "Aunt Marge." Marge and her husband, Larry, were originally from a farm family in Rochelle, IL. They spent a few years living in the same apartment building as my folks on the far south side of Chicago in a neighborhood called Pullman. They all became very good friends. When "Aunt Marge" and "Uncle Larry" returned to the Rochelle area, my family visited them on their farm for a week at a time during the summer. Those were wonderful times and wonderful memories. "Aunt Marge" was always upbeat and had a great sense of humor. She used to call me "Katy-Did." I thought that was sweet until I found out years later that a Katy–did was a bug similar to a grasshopper! I have carried on with the recipe and make the Potato Salad for special occasions, backyard barbeques, picnics, and luncheons. All the while I'm preparing the ingredients I can't help but think back to the laughter and good times we had with "Aunt Marge."

AUNT MARGE'S POTATO SALAD

INGREDIENTS

2-3 lbs. Yukon Gold or red potatoes

6 or more hard boiled eggs

1/2 - 1 cup diced celery

1/2 cup chopped red onion

1/3 cup chopped green onion

1/2 jar mayonnaise (one quart size, preferably Dukes brand)

1 1/2 tablespoons yellow mustard

1 teaspoon sugar

1 tablespoon red vinegar

1/4 cup milk

Parsley

Paprika

Salt and pepper to taste

PREPARATION

Boil potatoes in their jackets in salted water until just cooked through—don't over cook. Peel and cut potatoes into 1 inch cubes. Chop eggs, leaving one egg whole for garnishing. Add celery, onions, and a little chopped parsley. Mix well 5 remaining ingredients together in another bowl and gently fold into potatoes and eggs. Taste the salad and add more salt and pepper to taste. Garnish with the remaining egg cut into wedges and placed in a circle to resemble a flower. Use fresh parsley to create flower's stem and leaves. Sprinkle with paprika. (Nowadays folks don't peel red potatoes, so the option is yours.)

BARB'S BRAZILIAN BANANA BREAD

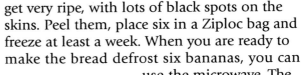

This is a recipe my mother used to make when we lived in Brazil (early 1940's) I have added my own touches so feel free to do the same. One of the

Barb Moore

"secrets" to the real banana flavor is this trick we learned from the Brazilian Ladies Club...Let your bananas get very ripe, with lots of black spots on the skins. Peel them, place six in a Ziploc bag and freeze at least a week. When you are ready to make the bread defrost six bananas, you can use the microwave. The bananas will look pretty bad and be surrounded by fluid. Have no fear...use everything in the bag, juice and all.

BRAZILIAN BANANA BREAD

INGREDIENTS

1/2 cup butter
(room temperature)

2 1/2 cups sugar

2 cups prefrozen bananas
(six soft) defrosted

3 1/4 cups flour
(sift with the baking powder)

2 teaspoons baking powder

2 teaspoons baking soda
(mixed with 2 tablespoons water)

2 teaspoons vanilla

2 eggs (slightly beaten)

1/2-cup sour cream

PREPARATION

Cream butter, add sugar a little at a time. Stir in bananas and beaten eggs. Add the flour/ baking powder mixture slowly. Add baking soda/ water, and then add vanilla and sour cream. Mix everything well.

PECAN TOPPING

3/4 stick butter (6 tablespoons); 1 1/2 cup chopped pecans; 3/4-1 cup dark brown sugar; 1 1/2 teaspoons vanilla

Mix in processor, adding pecans last (or mix by hand)

Beginning and Ending Tricks

Preheat oven to 350 degrees. Turn 9x13 pan upside down. Center a piece of foil long enough to cover pan shiny side down. Fold down sides and corners to fit the pan. Remove foil, turn pan over, and slide shaped foil into place. Place 2 tablespoons butter in pan, place foiled pan in oven couple of minutes, spread melted butter with brush or wadded wax paper over foil surface.

Put 1/2 pecan topping on bottom of buttered pan; spread banana mixture, top with remaining pecan topping. Bake for 50-60 minutes. Cool cake and then invert while covering cake with a cookie sheet. (Turn upside down) Remove the foil, and using a plate or another cookie sheet return right side up.

BECKI'S CRANBERRY SALAD

Vicki writes: "This recipe is from my recipe-sharing buddy, Becki. She's a friend I have had since my early 20's. We have had the same interest in cooking and exploring new recipes. We used to entertain each other with making new recipes on Saturday nights when we didn't have dates. Many were keepers and we had a great time doing it. We still share recipes today even though we are many states away from each other. The following is one of her recipes that I always make around the holidays as it is colorful and is always a hit."

Vicki

BECKI'S
CRANBERRY
SALAD

INGREDIENTS

1 – 1 1/2 cup sugar

1 lb. fresh cranberries

16 oz crushed pineapple
(drain 1/3 – 1/2 juice off)

Handful of coconut

1 apple (golden delicious
gives color

Zest of one orange

Chopped nuts

PREPARATION

Put cranberries in blender on chop. Chop fruits coarsely. Combine all ingredients in a serving bowl. The recipe develops better flavor if refrigerated for awhile.

Freezes well.

BRUSSELS SPROUTS & ARTICHOKE CASSEROLE

Carol Dallas is one of the first friends I made when relocating to the Atlanta area. We were introduced by a mutual friend, Barbe Ratcliffe, who writes in the Life Lessons section of this book. The more I spent time with Carol, the more I realized what a truly spiritual and grounded person she is. Professionally she is an intuitive coach and specializes in Mind, Body, Brain, and Spirit Integration. Her web site is www.brainspirit.com. Enjoy her commentary and her recipe.

Carol Dallas

"In the South, covered dish dinners are the height of a culinary experience. Meats, salads, casseroles, desserts galore, and fresh vegetables (home grown many of the times). Most dishes are guilty pleasures full of cheese, sugar, bread crumbs, mayonnaise and a host of other ingredients that we all try to leave off these days but love to eat at somebody else's table. Half the fun is finding something scrumptious that you just have to get the recipe for and badger whoever brought it until she coughs it up.

I spent nine years as the organist/choir director of the Methodist church in a small town in middle Georgia and we took every opportunity to host a covered dish supper. I have many fond memories of eating like a pig and chasing down recipes afterwards. This dish is one of those great surprises that had everybody charged up. I have fixed it many times over the years, including for a brother who hates brussels sprouts but gobbled up his share. It's quick, easy and you will be the heroine of the meal. (And yes, brussels sprouts has an "s" on the end of the word.)

"By the way, I was watching a Masterpiece Theater program about the English woman, Mrs. Beaton, who wrote a definitive guide to cooking and household management back in the Victorian era. Evidently, recipes before then were written down in no particular order. She said it was frustrating to find out halfway through that she needed seven partridges or whatever, so she devised the method we use now of listing all the ingredients at the beginning before the instructions."

BRUSSELS SPROUTS AND ARTICHOKE CASSEROLE RECIPE ON THE NEXT PAGE

BRUSSELS SPROUTS AND ARTICHOKE CASSEROLE

INGREDIENTS

1 pkg. frozen brussels sprouts, cooked till fork tender and drained. Can be left whole, but I like to cut them in half when they're done.

1 can (14 oz.) artichoke hearts, drained. Quarter them if you buy whole ones and do not buy the marinated ones.

2/3 cup mayonnaise

1/2 teaspoon celery salt

1/4 cup parmesan cheese

2 tablespoons butter, melted

2 tablespoons lemon juice

1/4 cup sliced almonds

PREPARATION

Combine cooked sprouts and drained artichoke hearts in a casserole. Combine all other ingredients and pour over the top.

Cook at 425 degrees for 10 minutes.

CHICKEN CORDON BLEU

This is one of the first recipes we had at our Gourmet Club that we started over 30 years ago. The club began with five couples; two are still involved. We have continued on with new couples. One of our members always cooked our gourmet meal while we had wine and appetizers. Inspired by them, I always want to be ready with everything to join in the fun whenever they come to my house. This continues to be one of my favorite recipes.

Dorothy Warren

CHICKEN
CORDON
BLEU

INGREDIENTS

4 whole chicken breasts, split, boned and skinned

8 – 1 oz slices cooked ham

8 – 1 oz slices Swiss cheese

3 tablespoons minced fresh parsley

1/4 teaspoon pepper

1 egg beaten

1/2 cup milk

1/2 cup fine dry bread crumbs

1/4 cup margarine

1 – 10 3/4 oz. can mushroom soup, undiluted

1 – 8 oz. carton sour cream

1/3 cup dry Sherry

1 lb. sautéed sliced mushrooms

PREPARATION

Place each chicken breast on sheet of waxed paper. Flatten to 1/4 inch thickness, using a meat mallet or rolling pin. Place one slice of cheese and ham in center of each prepared chicken breast. Roll up lengthwise and secure with wooden picks.

Combine egg and milk. Dip each chicken breast in egg and milk mixture. Coat with bread crumbs, parsley and pepper mixture. Cover and chill one hour.

Melt butter in heavy skillet, brown chicken on all sides. Put in greased baking dish. Reserve drippings in skillet.

Add remaining ingredients to reserved drippings and stir well. Pour sauce over chicken, bake uncovered at 350 degrees for 40 to 45 minutes or till done.

This meal is even great the next day.

CHOCOLATE ESPRESSO CHEESECAKE

A friend of mine from the Northwest writes: "We raised our family and lived for 34 years on a small island close to Seattle. The little local newspaper had a cook-off every year with fun prizes for the winners. This recipe won in 1985 and I have made it often since."

CHOCOLATE
ESPRESSO
CHEESECAKE

(From the coffee capital of the country – Seattle)

INGREDIENTS

24 oz. cream cheese

26 chocolate wafers – crushed

2 tablespoons sugar

1/4 cup butter – melted

1 (12 oz) pkg semisweet chocolate chips

4 tablespoons Espresso coffee

1 cup sugar

2 tablespoons flour

3 eggs

2 egg yolks

1 cup heavy cream

PREPARATION

Let cream cheese soften in a large bowl. Blend chocolate wafer crumbs, 2 tablespoons sugar and butter in a medium bowl. Press over bottom and halfway up side of a lightly buttered 9 inch spring form pan, prechilled.

Melt chocolate chips in a double boiler. Beat cream cheese until just smooth. Add sugar gradually, beating until light and fluffy. Sprinkle flour over mixture and blend thoroughly. Add eggs and yolks, one at a time, beating well after each one. Beat in melted chocolate, coffee and cream at low speed. Pour into pan.

Bake at 325 - 350 degrees on top rack for 1 hour. Turn off oven and let cake remain with door closed for 40 minutes. Remove and cool completely on rack. Refrigerate several hours. Garnish with dark chocolate shavings.

CHOCOLATE FUDGE SAUCE

I first met Maria Tillotson over twenty years ago while attending a Corporate Relocation Conference. She was presenting a training program on behalf of her company.

Maria Tillotson

When she happened to mention that she lived in Sedona, Arizona, I knew we were kindred spirits. We visit her area at least once a year and I consider it my Heaven on Earth. How fortunate is she to actually live there and in a truly gorgeous home that backs up to the famous red rocks. As often as possible my husband and I pay her and Doug a visit to catch up on family and industry news.

When I approached her for a contribution to this book, she responded immediately—that's the kind of person she is. I really admire her. Here's her recipe for a yummy fudge sauce:

"This recipe has been an all time favorite of my family and one that has never lost its popularity. When we first moved to Southern California in 1953, as a young mother, I was blessed to develop a friendship with the wife of a gentleman who worked for my husband's father in the insulation business. My dear friend's name was Georgia. Although she was several years older than me, her children were very close in age to our youngsters. She was truly my mentor in so many, many ways. I looked upon her with great respect and admiration while learning some priceless things from her motherly role. She was indeed an excellent cook and I cherish a number of recipes that she had shared with me over the years. This particular one became a real favorite in our household and remains so even today, some 50 years later."

CHOCOLATE FUDGE SAUCE RECIPE ON NEXT PAGE

CHOCOLATE FUDGE SAUCE

INGREDIENTS

1 tablespoon real butter

1 cube (1oz) unsweetened Baker's chocolate

1/3 cup white sugar

Real cream

PREPARATION

In a small heavy skillet (omelet type pan), slowly melt butter. Add chocolate stirring till it also melts. The sugar should be added a little bit at a time, while stirring constantly as the mixture begins to thicken. The sugar/chocolate does not appear to be melting, but once you add "cream" very slowly (pouring a little bit at a time) in the center, like magic, the mixture becomes a smooth sauce! The amount of cream depends on how thin you want the sauce to become. The secret is not to hurry and continuous stirring is a key to the success. Once you serve the sauce over ice cream, the cooling makes it a bit chewy which is a part of its character. Any leftovers can be stored in a small microwave container and refrigerated. The sauce is simple to restore by warming in a microwave for only a few seconds. As it warms, you will want to add more cream for thinning and stir well until the mixture becomes smooth once again. A rubber spatula is a perfect choice for preparing and/or reheating this sauce.

CHRISTMAS TIME TREATS

Ray Horvath

I attended a Hungarian Catholic Grammar School many years ago (I will be 79 in September). Christmas was always full of special activities. As young as we were, our parents allowed us to stay up for the Midnight Mass Celebration. The beautiful ceremony was preceded by a procession of the school children singing Latin and English verses to hymns. The nuns sang Latin hymns from the choir loft as the boys and girls carried lighted white candles down the aisle towards the altar. Some of the altar boys were dressed in outfits that were similar to those worn by Cardinals. Others were attired in the traditional black and white altar boys' outfits. The girls all had special white dresses with large white bows connected to a headpiece.

Special though the memory of Midnight Mass is to me, the most cherished memory I have during that time is about my Aunt Emma. She lived a few short blocks from the school. Occasionally I went to her house for lunch or a short visit. Every Christmas Aunt Emma made Beiglis — a Hungarian cookie dessert. It was similar to a jellyroll but in cookie form — a nut roll sliced in 1/2 inch thick pieces. They were awesome. I usually wanted six or more — no one could eat just one, especially me. Beiglis are made especially at Christmas and are considered to be a Hungarian baking tradition for more than 100 years.

BEIGLIS [HUNGARIAN NUT COOKIES] RECIPE ON THE NEXT PAGE

BEIGLIS
HUNGARIAN
NUT COOKIES

FOR THE DOUGH

1 envelope dry yeast
or 1 square of yeast

1/4 cup warm milk

2 sticks unsalted butter,
cubed

4 beaten egg yolks

1/2 pint half and half

4 cups flour

1 teaspoon granulated
sugar

3/4 teaspoon salt

1 teaspoon vanilla

FOR NUT FILLING

1 1/2 cups granulated
sugar

1 lb. finely chopped
walnuts

4 egg whites stiffly beaten

1 teaspoon vanilla

Pinch of cinnamon

1 egg white

1 tablespoon water

PREPARATION:

Dissolve the yeast in the milk. Melt butter. Mix butter with egg yolks in a large bowl. In another bowl sift flour, sugar, cinnamon and salt together. Combine yeast mixture with butter, and egg yolks, half and half, and then add the flour mixture. Stir until the mixture is smooth. Form into 3 balls and refrigerate overnight.

FOR THE FILLING:

Mix together nuts and sugar; add vanilla. Fold into beaten egg whites. Use 1 – 1 1/4 cups filling per roll.

Divide the dough into three pieces. Roll one piece of dough at a time on a lightly floured board and form a rectangle that is about 1/4 inch thick.. (always keep the remaining dough covered so it doesn't dry out.) Spread 1/3 of the walnut filling on top of the dough and leave about an inch of plain dough at each edge. Roll the dough to form a log (jelly roll fashion). Press ends to seal, then place seam side down on a parchment lined baking sheet. Repeat with the remaining dough and filling. Let the rolls rest in a warm place for about 1 hour to rise. Make an egg wash by beating the egg white and water. Repeat the process to create the remaining 2 rolls. After the rolls have risen, brush with the egg wash.

Preheat oven at 325 degrees. Bake the rolls about 45 minutes to an hour or until they turn a deep golden brown. Dust with confectioners' sugar when ready to serve and cut into 1/2 inch pieces.

As an alternative or as an additional filling option, a can of poppy seed filling can be used. Both are absolutely delicious.

The rolls can be refrigerated for up to 2 weeks or frozen for several months.

COLD FARRO or COLD RISOTTO

Aldo is the son of my grandparents' friends who emigrated from Italy shortly after the turn of the century. He frequently travels back to visit and brags about his cousin

Rosanna Magnani

Rosanna's culinary skills. He was kind enough to approach her on my behalf and then translated into English her verbal instructions. Cold farro is a great Tuscan dish, popular in the summertime. He warns that getting farro and condiriso will be your challenge. He got his through the internet. You can simply do a search for Condiriso and several sites come up offering the product. However, there are so many ethnic stores and world markets established in local communities these days, it may not be all that hard. He suggests adjusting to taste by adding or deleting items. Here is Rosanna's recipe:

Aldo's note: Condiriso (from "condire riso") is a mixture of vegetables in variable quantities (peppers, cucumbers, carrots, green and black olive rings, capers, turnips, fennel, artichokes, peas) in rice oil, wine vinegar, salt, and some spices. It comes in small jars not unlike those containing pickled vegetable (not to be used as substitute).

Farro is a primitive wheat which is still grown in certain parts of the world, most specifically in the Garfagnana area in Northern Tuscany. It's cultivation and marketing is closely controlled like Chianti Classico wine. Also called "emmer wheat". Check this site for a good description: http://en.wikipedia.org/wiki/Emmer

COLD FARRO
or
COLD RISOTTO

INGREDIENTS AND PREPARATION

In a large pot add 4 quarts of water and a pinch of salt; bring to a boil. When boiling, add package of farro (500 grams.) Cook for 30 minutes then check farro for al dente texture. If too hard, cook another 5-10 minutes. Do not over cook!

Drain farro and water in colander as you would spaghetti or rice. Place farro in a large bowl (stainless steel or porcelain) and allow it to cool to room temperature.

ADDING CONDIRISO:

Open 3-4 jars of condiriso and drain juice. Pour condiriso into the farro. Into the farro add 1-2 jars of heart of palm of artichokes (cut up and drained). Cut up 1/4 lb of either soft Asiago cheese or Swiss cheese. Add a can of tuna, drained, if desired. Add 1-3 cans of mushrooms, drained. Add extra virgin oil and salt to taste. Stir contents and serve or may be refrigerated and served cold.

COMPARATIVELY SPEAKING

I grew up with this troublesome habit of always comparing myself to others. Sometimes it would work to my advantage when I admired something in another person. A sense of humor, kindness to others, positive attitude towards life, calm, spiritual, etc. were positive attributes I would try to emulate. That's the good kind of comparison. I like to think it made me a better person.

Cathy Horvath

Then there's the other kind. I have always compared myself to other girls in my class who were cuter, smarter, sweeter, prettier, richer, and, of course, more popular. When I shared this with my Mom, she would turn it around and tell me I hurt her feelings because that meant she didn't raise a cute, smart, pretty, popular daughter and we certainly weren't rich. From then on I kept my feelings to myself.

The habit continued into my adult life. I didn't have a body like the models in the magazines or movie stars. I continued to compare myself to gals I saw here and there or knew from the neighborhood, church, PTA, you name it. Comparison opportunities were everywhere. My hair didn't look as good as hers. Boy can she dance—she's got all the moves down. She is a lot smarter than I—why can't I be that smart? I wish I could sing like she does; my voice is good but untrained. She is so intellectual—I wish I could be like that. She sure does a good job raising her children—so attentive, loving, and caring. I could/should do better. Wow, can she cook—doesn't need a cookbook like I do. She is so athletic. I can't do a darn thing in sports. Afraid of water, never saw a ball game—there's a whole part of life I have missed out on.

Then the light bulb turned on. It didn't happen overnight. It took little messages I received from many different sources. Self help books like *I'm Okay, You're Okay* by Thomas A. Harris and so many others I read that were similar and some with an even more spiritual connotation. Through all the years of listening to speakers, attending seminars, and reading oh so many books, it took my Guardian Angels "to put it to me straight." God doesn't create imperfect beings. Our souls are a reflection of God's Divinity and our light shines as individuals with free wills. How boring a world this would be if we all looked alike and acted alike! A world of Stepford Wives! Each of us has a contribution to make to the world, a life purpose so to speak. Big or small, we all make contributions to the world. That makes us special in our own way. Regardless of my skin color, freckles, body shape, skills (and we all have them to some extent) hair style, my walk, the way I dress—everything about me defines who I am and why I am special. I have an obligation to God to honor the individual He created as unique as each snowflake. I'm okay now; are you okay?

COUNTRY STYLE MACARONI AND MEAT

This recipe is about as old as my marriage (51 years). The card it is typed on has yellowed. I have lost count as to how many times I have served it over the years with no complaints from my family. I used to serve it with a small tossed salad on the side. But if you are short on time and need a one pot meal that has a little bit of everything, this is your dish.

Cathy Horvath

COUNTRY STYLE
MACARONI
AND MEAT

INGREDIENTS

1 pkg. cooked elbow macaroni

1/4 cup butter or margarine

2 medium onions, chopped

1 clove garlic minced

1 1/4 lbs. ground beef

1 small jar pimentos, chopped

1 #2 can red kidney beans

1 cup cooked peas

Salt and pepper to taste

PREPARATION

Melt butter or margarine; add onions, garlic and beef. Cook over medium heat until beef is browned. Add macaroni and remaining ingredients. Mix well and heat to serving temperature on top of stove or in a lightly greased casserole in a 325 degree oven for 25 to 30 minutes or until all ingredients have blended.

CRITICISM

Have you noticed lately that judgment and criticism seem to be part of our everyday lives? The older I get the more aware I am of this phenomenon.

Cathy Horvath

Simon Cowell has made a fortune and has gained global recognition doing it. We criticize parenting skills, how others lead their lives, what some folks do with their money, how they dress, etc. Sometimes, I think, criticisms just creep into our conversations without realizing what we're doing.

I'm a type A personality and strive for perfection in every thing I do. It's an unrealistic pressure I put on myself, I know. I've been that way ever since I was a kid growing up in a family that expected nothing less from me. There are a lot of theories out there about that. A famous actress once said that perfection was her way of seeking and receiving love from her father that she didn't get any other way. I've been on the receiving end of criticism my whole life, especially raising my four children and during my career as a corporate executive. Everyone had an opinion or a complaint. I struggled to satisfy everyone's needs or issues. I once had a boss tell me "Don't tell me what's wrong without giving me a solution." Smart man! I quickly learned to turn a criticism into a request from the critic for a solution. That helped in several instances.

The worst experience I had and the one I will take to my grave is a criticism I received from my father. Since my folks retired and lived several hundred miles away, we frequently spoke by phone. I would update them on our family life. Besides the good report cards and athletic achievements, I would share the typical trials and tribulations that parents experience when raising four kids. During one of those weekly conversations, Dad commented that the struggles we were having with our children were because they were looking for the love they never received from their Mother. That cut to the core! And I really didn't deserve it. He didn't live with us; he lived out of state. He couldn't have known what was going on in our home on a daily basis. He just didn't know. His comment taught me a wonderful lesson: never judge or criticize unless you know all the circumstances, and even then—don't judge.

When my husband and I visited friends in Tucson who had recently moved from the Chicago area, they proudly toured us through each room of their new house. That was more than thirty years ago but to this day I remember a plaque that hung on their family room wall. It was an old Native American saying: "Let he who would criticize me walk first a mile in my moccasins." Doesn't that say it all?

DAD'S ZUCCHINI BREAD

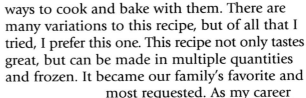

When we lived in the Western suburbs of Chicago, we planted a huge garden in our backyard every spring. We had about 1 1/2 acres of land so there was plenty of room for all varieties

Ray Horvath

of vegetables. One of our favorites was zucchini. We learned early on how prolific those plants are. We soon became experts in the many ways to cook and bake with them. There are many variations to this recipe, but of all that I tried, I prefer this one. This recipe not only tastes great, but can be made in multiple quantities and frozen. It became our family's favorite and most requested. As my career began to take off, my baking decreased. So my husband Ray took over and from then on, it became known as Dad's Zucchini Bread.

DAD'S
ZUCCHINI
BREAD

INGREDIENTS

2 cups sugar

1 cup vegetable oil

3 eggs

3 cups flour

1 teaspoon salt

3 teaspoons cinnamon

1/2 teaspoon nutmeg

1/2 teaspoon baking powder

1 teaspoon baking soda

2 teaspoons vanilla

2 cups pared and coarsely grated zucchini

1 cup chopped walnuts

(optional: 1 cup raisins)

PREPARATION

Beat sugar and oil until smooth. Add eggs, one at a time mixing well after each addition. Combine dry ingredients and add to first mixture. Then gently stir in vanilla, zucchini and walnuts. Pour into 2 loaf pans that have been greased and floured.

Bake at 325 degrees for 1 hour or until tester comes out clean.

DARLENE'S LIFE LESSON

While between jobs in the late 90's, I received a call from Darlene Marcus in Irvine, CA. and CEO of her own corporate relocation company. She invited me to visit her the following week. She had an idea and according to her, I was the perfect person to talk to about it. Darlene had an outstanding reputation in the Relocation Industry as an innovator and leader. I didn't ask another question. I made the trip. We talked about her idea and she hired me as Director of her company's newly created web site division. I didn't even know back then what the World Wide Web was all about. Darlene understood that but she also knew that I love to learn new things and to be challenged to grow.

Several weeks after settling into my new office in Naperville, IL. and getting started on this new opportunity, I received a call from her. "How are you? How are you doing? Do you have everything you need? Are you happy?"

"Am I happy?" I've never had a boss ask me that! I admit I was a little skeptical. But I responded very honestly. When you read her life lesson, you will understand why she made that call. Now I do too. In all the years I have been employed, with all the bosses I've ever had, no one ranks up there with Darlene. She is ethical, spiritual, honest and just very nice. I count her as a blessing in my life and a wonderful friend.

DARLENE'S LIFE LESSON:

In my mid 20's I was transferred by my company to New York City. I might as well have been transferred to London. It was so different from Los Angeles and its surrounding suburbs. New York City was big, crowded and the people seemed indifferent to anyone and everyone. The rich were visible in their limousines and uptown, fashionable apartments. Everyone else just seemed to blend into the surrounding concert.

When I first moved to the city I found an apartment over a restaurant on the Upper East Side. It was a great location but one I really could not afford. So after a few months I was able to share a two bedroom apartment with a new found friend. The apartment was in a welfare hotel located in Mid-Town Manhattan. Across the street stood a clothing factory. Many of the old factory buildings were being converted into lofts. A few blocks away, prostitutes owned the streets. While living in the welfare hotel I met some incredible people. Without question no one, including themselves, would claim that they were the "beautiful people" of New York City. Most of them had lived their lives and were just hanging around with no real purpose or focus anymore. Some were still trying to survive in the city. Others, like me and my roommate, couldn't afford the expense of the city so we had to find cheaper housing and compromise some of our expectations.

One Saturday morning I stopped to talk with a woman who was sitting on the front stoop of the hotel. We had been talking for about five minutes when I introduced myself. I then asked her what her name was. She started crying. A little cautiously I asked her what was wrong. I certainly didn't mean to insult her. She indicated to me that I was the first person to ask her name in a very long time. I was stunned. Here this elderly woman, living alone in a welfare hotel, had not had anyone interested in knowing her name for some time. I learned that she had been in the hospital for several weeks and had just been released. I wondered if anyone came to visit her during her illness. Strange as it was, I never saw her again after that encounter, but the lesson she taught me that day has stayed with me ever since.

As my career was taking off, I was privileged to live in a place where most upward mobile people won't even spend an afternoon, let alone live there. I realized that no matter what title you had, where you worked or the money you made, you can't ignore the simple human need to connect with people and take an interest in them. I also became acutely aware that it doesn't take much to be a blessing to someone: a smile, a kind word, a fifteen minute conversation. As I was fortunate to excel in the business world, I always tried to remember that lesson. Throughout my career I tried to treat people at all levels with respect, to take time to listen to them, and realize we are all valuable in God's eyes. I wanted to be a blessing to people. That philosophy has served me well throughout my life and I was blessed to learn the lesson early.

Oh by the way, the woman's name was Eleanor.

DEATH BY CHOCOLATE

Mary Ann Williams

I was born and raised in a very small town in central Missouri called Fortuna. I went to grade school there but when it came time for high school, I went to a consolidated school in Tipton which drew from nearby small communities. I entered Tipton High School in 1951 not knowing anyone. By the end of the year I was "buddies" with four girls. These four girls had friends that were in the 8th grade so I became acquainted with them also. By my second year, our group had increased to 12 girl "buddies." Of course, this was a "click" only we didn't know that back in the 50's. We soon named our group The Dirty Dozen of Tipton or The DDTs. (Tipton was a farming community and the farmers of that date used DDT to control weeds.)

We continued this friendship throughout high school. We were cheerleaders. We were involved in school plays. We held fund raisers for various school projects, and enjoyed many sleepovers. When I graduated, I went to college for one year and then married my high school sweetheart Gene. The DDTs still kept in touch but as more married, more left Tipton. Gene and I moved to Kansas City and over the years, some of us stayed close and some of us lost touch.

Eight years ago one of our group decided to get us all back together, so she arranged a reunion for a weekend at Branson, MO. All but one came. Each year since, we have met in Branson. Since we are all retired, our reunions have extended to four or five days. Over the years we have lost three husbands and cancer has touched every family but one. We have been there to support each other through hard times. Because we have had a long history with each other, there is a very strong bond among us. Another factor that has kept us so close is that each girl of the original 12 has had the same mate. No divorce, which we feel is either a result of our times (the fifties) or just stupidity

Four years ago I had the gals submit recipes and I made a cookbook for everyone for the next reunion. I went through the cookbook and am submitting a recipe we all love. Of course, it is full of calories!

DEATH BY CHOCOLATE RECIPE ON THE NEXT PAGE

DEATH
BY
CHOCOLATE

INGREDIENTS

Brownie mix
(family size 19.8 oz)

1 pkg. Jell-O no bake silk
chocolate pie dessert filling

10 (1 oz.) Heath or Skor
candy bars

1 cup pecans (chopped)

1 carton Cool Whip (12 oz.)

1/4 to 1/2 cup Kahlua
(optional)

PREPARATION

Bake brownies per package directions. While warm from
the oven, punch holes in brownies and pour Kahlua over
top. Mix chocolate dessert per package directions. Crush
candy into small pieces. Crumble half of brownies in bottom
of trifle dish or large clear glass bowl. Layer half of chocolate
dessert over brownies. Add half of candy bars, half of nuts
and half of Cool Whip. Repeat layers ending with Cool
Whip. Sprinkle some candy crumbs over the top.

NOTE: Kahula and or nuts can be eliminated. Also, 3
boxes of either cook or instant Jell-O chocolate pudding
mix can be substituted.

DEBRA'S POTATO CASSEROLE

Debra offered this potato recipe recalled from her childhood days. We worked together in Chicago for several years until she and her husband decided to move to Cary, N.C. We were kindred spirits in that our work ethics were the same, and so we've stayed connected even though we've both moved to different parts of the country. Here's Debra's memory and recipe:

Debra

"I love to celebrate the Easter holiday and I have several reasons to rejoice: there aren't a lot of presents to buy and wrap; it's not an over-commercialized holiday; it's a time of rebirth and renewal; it means that spring is just around the corner; and then there are all those adorable chocolate bunnies to eat!

My family celebrated the Easter holiday in all the traditional ways. We decorated Easter eggs. We assembled and then hid Easter baskets. And, of course, we went to church. But to me, the very best part of the holiday was coming home after church to a huge and scrumptious brunch. The food served was a wonderful way to wrap up the holiday, and since it was a brunch, Mom didn't have to spend the whole day in the kitchen preparing the feast. The menu varied a bit each year, but there were a few staples, such as: ham, hard boiled eggs (colored, naturally), polish sausage, potatoes, asparagus and a lamb cake. I'd like to share with you Mom's very easy recipe for the potatoes, and just maybe, it could become a small part of one of your family's traditions, too. Thanks, Mom."

DEBRA'S POTATO
CASSEROLE
RECIPE
ON THE
NEXT PAGE

DEBRA'S POTATO CASSEROLE

INGREDIENTS

2 pounds frozen, plain diced potatoes (like Ore-Ida. Thaw in refrigerator for use)

1 can cream of mushroom soup

1 pound shredded cheddar cheese (your preference, mild or sharp)

1/2 cup green onions

1 pint sour cream

4 tablespoons (1/2 stick) butter, melted

1 teaspoon salt

PREPARATION:

Heat oven to 350 degrees. Spray a 9" x12" baking dish with non-stick cooking spray (like Pam).

Mix soup, onion, sour cream, salt and melted butter together in a large bowl.

Gently fold in diced potatoes and cheese.

Pour into baking dish and bake uncovered at 350 degrees for one (1) hour.

Remove from oven and serve.

DO YOU HAVE THE RIGHT IDOL TO IMPERSONATE?

Cathy Horvath

As I was getting dressed this morning, brushing my hair, and putting on my makeup, my thoughts somehow turned to the runway models, television stars, and movie stars. I looked in the mirror and decided I never have nor will I ever resemble what the media declares "high fashion." Don't get me wrong, my friends have declared me a "fashionista" because I love to wear pretty clothes and am always certain my hair and makeup are just right. I'm a Leo—what can I say? But the interesting part of this experience was that my Guardian Angels kicked in with the following thoughts:

It is amazing to us to watch humanity identify with specific people in the limelight. Take runway models, for instance. Their bodies are not of average size; their faces are made up in an exaggerated manner; their hair is tossed, curled, colored, and twisted in the most surreal mode. We understand this is done purposefully to attain a so-called 'fashion statement.' Fashion is a multi-billion dollar industry. The problem arises when men and women of all ages desire to replicate those looks in order to be 'fashionable.' A reasonable adaptation of the clothing styles for the season usually shows up in department stores and boutiques later on. The problem is, not everyone is bone thin and very tall in order to carry off these looks. It is sad to see both men and women belittle their bodies by wearing styles that are not complimentary to them only because it's the style. Common sense suggestion one: honor your body by wearing what is appropriate for you with a bit of fashion flare—be it color, fabric or pattern. When you honor your body you honor the God that created it.

The same goes for the countless media and movie stars that are idolized, revered, and mimicked simply because of their celebrity. It is appalling to us that the unethical and immoral values that these prominent figures display are considered acceptable and mimicked throughout the world. The same is true for your political leaders, no matter the country. Your society has things upside down. There are countless souls on earth that are caring, generous, honest and hard working. Look around you—they are your neighbors, your teachers, your Emergency Medical Teams, volunteers, nurses, family members —you get the idea. These folks deserve recognition and copying. Common sense suggestion two: Honor those who walk the path to Heaven. Honor yourself by going deep within yourself and finding your God self there. Let God express through you and set an example for others. Once you do that, others will notice and be attracted to your words and deeds. You therefore have planted a God seed and have made a huge difference in the world. God be with you on your path."

EASY APPLE SLICES

My friend Marianne gave me this recipe one day after she and I and our children spent an afternoon together at her home. There was no such thing as meeting for lunch back in the '60's—especially with six or eight children to handle. We had more fun taking turns at each other's house and sending the kids to the backyard with their own bags of peanut butter and jelly sandwiches, cookies, and a pitcher of Kool-Aid. Well, back to the recipe....this is so easy and makes such a large batch of apple slices that is does well for bake sales, pot luck suppers or "just because."

Cathy Horvath

EASY
APPLE
SLICES

INGREDIENTS FOR CRUST

4 cups sifted flour

1 1/2 cups shortening

4 egg yolks

2 tablespoons lemon juice

About 8-12 tablespoons iced water

INGREDIENTS FOR FILLING

3 cans apples, drained well and sliced thin or 8 cups of thinly sliced fresh apples

1 1/2 cups brown sugar

1 1/2 cups granulated sugar

1/2 teaspoon nutmeg

1 1/2 teaspoons cinnamon

PREPARATION

CRUST: Combine ingredients and roll layers between two sheets of parchment paper cut to fit the bottom of a 15x10 jelly roll pan but leaving a little extra on all sides for crimping with the top crust. Take care to add the water slowly so that the dough is moist and can be rolled out easily. You may not need all that water. Place dough in the bottom of the baking pan.

FILLING: Combine ingredients. Pour into the baking pan and dot with a tablespoon of butter cut into small pieces. Moisten edges of bottom crust, lay top crust over the apple mixture and crimp. Wash crust with beaten egg white, sprinkle with a little granulated sugar and make air vents with the prong of a fork. Bake at 375 degrees for 50 minutes to an hour. Keep checking the crust until it is light golden brown. If served warm with vanilla ice cream on top, it is a most delightful dessert!

EASY POUND CAKE

One of my favorite ladies is a former preschool and kindergarten teacher and has volunteered at a local hospital for many years. Kindness and generosity is a way of life for her. I am honored to include one of her recipes. She writes:

"A wonderful lady gave this recipe to me. I worked with her in the 80's. We liked to talk about food and share recipes. There are many pound cake recipes in culinary land but this one is a little different. It has a wonderful flavor and is so easy to prepare."

EASY
POUND
CAKE

INGREDIENTS

6 eggs

2 sticks butter

3 cups flour
[sifted 3 times]

3 cups sugar

1 teaspoon vanilla

1/2 pint whipping cream

PREPARATION

Preheat oven to 325 degrees, grease and flour Bundt pan. Cream butter and sugar together. Add eggs one at a time. Then add flour alternately with the whipping cream. Add vanilla.

Pour into pan and bake for about 1 hour and 10-15 minutes [total].

Cool in pan 10 minutes before removing. Serve with Cool Whip or ice cream.

EILEEN'S CINNAMON COFFEE CAKE

I took a brief break from writing to have lunch. Instead of grabbing something from the refrigerator and standing at the counter to eat a quick lunch, I decided to sit at our kitchen table and read our local newspaper while snacking on leftovers. To my delight, one section of the paper featured family traditions for the upcoming Easter holiday. A tradition shared by Lynne Riley, Fulton County (GA.) Commissioner brought a smile to my face. I contacted Mrs. Riley and received permission to print the recipe that she shared.

Eileen Riley

Mrs. Riley tells that her daughter Eileen, 22 at the time, has become quite a cook, and pitches in to make the batter for the breakfast treat the night before she bakes it. Imagine the delightful scent that wafts through the Riley household Easter morning as this cake comes out of the oven.

They both agree that this recipe is a wonderful offering on Christmas or other special occasions as well.

EILEEN'S CINNAMON COFFEE CAKE

INGREDIENTS AND PREPARATION

2 cups plain flour

1 cup sugar

1/2 cup brown sugar

1 teaspoon baking soda

1 teaspoon baking powder

1/2 teaspoon salt

1 teaspoon cinnamon

Mix all the above ingredients together and add:

1 cup buttermilk

2/3 cup butter, melted

2 large eggs

Beat at medium speed for 3 minutes. Pour into a greased and floured 13x9 pan.

Prepare and sprinkle on top:

1/2 cup brown sugar

1 cup chopped nuts (optional)

1 teaspoon cinnamon

Cover cake, refrigerate over night. Next morning, uncover and bake at 350 degrees for 30 minutes or until done.

ELENA'S BROCCOLI PUFF

It's quite remarkable that I have a recipe from my Aunt Elena (actually we called her Zia which is Aunt in Italian.) You see, Zia was a career woman all the way into her 80's. Sadly, she passed away in her 91st year. She and my Uncle Victor never had children, so my siblings and I were her surrogate family. She was a kind and generous woman who was admired and respected by all who had the privilege of knowing her. She and my uncle retired to Mountain Home, AR. in their 60's. Not one to slow down, she kept on working because she thrived on the camaraderie with office associates and the

Cathy Horvath

opportunity to meet new people. She volunteered at the Chamber of Commerce and Baxter General Hospital. She was a member of the Business and Professional Women's Club. She traveled, took classes, shopped, and enjoyed many activities. What she didn't do was excel in the kitchen. Much to her chagrin, she struggled to make Jell-O when she had newly retired and made an attempt at being a Kitchen Diva. She got a whole lot better as the years passed, but never made it to the Diva status. But one recipe we all enjoyed during one holiday visit was her Broccoli Puff. So on June 15, 1983 she was proud and pleased to pass along the following recipe to me:

ELENA'S BROCCOLI PUFF

INGREDIENTS

2 (10 oz.) pkgs. chopped broccoli

3 eggs, separated

1 tablespoon all purpose flour

Pinch of ground nutmeg

1 cup mayonnaise

1/4 teaspoon garlic powder

1 tablespoon butter

1/4 teaspoon salt

1/4 teaspoon pepper

1/4 cup plus 1 tablespoon grated parmesan cheese

PREPARATION

Cook broccoli according to package directions. Drain well. Beat egg yolks, add flour, mixing well. Stir in nutmeg, mayonnaise, butter, salt, pepper, garlic and cheese. Add broccoli, mixing lightly. Beat egg whites (at room temperature) until stiff but not dry. Gently fold into broccoli mixture. Pour into a lightly buttered 9 inch square baking dish.

Bake at 350 degrees for 30 minutes. Cut into squares to serve. Serves 9

FAIRNESS HAS NOTHING TO DO WITH IT

Cathy Horvath

Several years ago, I received a call from a friend and business associate.. She was soft spoken, kind, and generous. I considered it an honor to be her friend. While attending a meeting out of state a few months prior, we shared our common beliefs in Angels and their contribution to our spiritual growth. She knew that I had learned to communicate with my Guardian Angels, so we had a lot to talk about. Along with other attendees, we stayed on a few extra days to lunch, shop, and just have fun. We had a delightful time sharing anecdotes about our jobs, families, and our lives in general. She was so proud of her son—they had a very tight bond and from all she had to say, he was certainly a great kid. Then there were references to her husband and their home. All good stuff. It was apparent that she led a happy, fulfilled life.

That's why it came as a shock when she called and told me her husband had left her and her son. He just walked out with no warning, no clues. He managed to wipe out their life savings and their son's college fund. Apparently he had a mistress and they were running away to pursue "the good life." Shattered and full of pain, she asked if I would please talk to my Angels about her situation and give her some guidance. "I am so hurt and upset. I just want to give him the divorce he wants and split our remaining assets down the middle. I just want to be fair and get on with my life," she said.

As much as I wanted to help a friend in need of guidance, I did not see myself as having the abilities she requested. I told her I communicate with my angels for my own purposes but that I couldn't take responsibility for the information I received on behalf of another. At her urging and with her permission, I asked my Angels to ask her Guardian Angels to help us both out.

And did they ever! I just sat at my computer, prayed for guidance and typed my heart out. I don't pay much attention to what comes through until I go back to correct typos. Here's the kicker: they said "fairness has nothing to do with this." "What?" I thought to myself. I thought Angels were always about fairness and fair play. Be nice, share, turn the other cheek—that's the Angelic way. Not so in this case.

They went on to explain: This man has done this sort of thing before and walked away with no retribution. Now he is doing it again. He needs to be held accountable for his actions or he will continue this routine until life catches up with him. If she gives in and sets him free with no responsibility for his actions, she is selling herself and God short. She is not honoring the person God created who deserves all the blessings that are owed her. She did nothing wrong. She must stand up for herself and her son and demand an appropriate resolution to the dissolution of the marriage and assets."

I printed this message out and mailed it to her. She was so grateful to our Angels and for the encouraging words. In the following months, their divorce became final. Her former husband was ordered to repay their son's college fund and their assets were divided but more so to her satisfaction than his. A few years later I learned he had indeed travelled to Hawaii and married and pulled the same trick on wife #3. This time he was bankrupt. My friend's career has escalated beyond her wildest dreams and, as predicted in the message, a very fine gentleman has come into her life. This time, the relationship is different. She is very much her own person. She puts her needs first and honors her Divinity.

FINDING MY SELF ESTEEM

Jerry is a dear friend and a well respected psychotherapist. Her life experiences have helped her go beyond her textbook degree and reach out to her clients because she understands. This is her life lesson she wishes to share:

Jerry Connor

"I grew up knowing I was on the smart side, but not too smart. I wasn't ugly, but not especially pretty either. I was very shy and quiet. My self-esteem wasn't totally lacking yet I certainly lacked confidence. What little I had disappeared after I married. What I didn't give my husband, he took. It wasn't until after my divorce that I began to find myself again.

When my children were in elementary school, the school counselor decided she would have speakers come in on Tuesday mornings during the month of February. I cannot recall three of the offerings. One, however, has stayed with me and is a wonderful tool I use to help others in the work that I do. Simply stated, it was a way to conceptualize how we form our self-esteem. I had never thought about that before. The underscoring message was that 'others' and 'family' did not matter as much as what 'I' knew about what I did. I have to know if my efforts were sincere, honest, well executed or not. Did I earn what I received or did I have a run of luck? I had found the first chunk of my self-esteem.

In my early forties, I went to graduate school. In one particular class, we had a group report to do. My group studied self-esteem in children. I cannot remember exactly what occurred during the research on the subject. I do remember that I found another chunk of my self esteem. (Maybe I was well received by my group-mates and/or I was gaining confidence in myself as I progressed through a learning experience that ended in a master's degree. Lord only knows you learn a lot about yourself when you study human behavior!)

It was an on-going, very slow process. I was in and out of psychotherapy sessions for the next decade. Although I can't recall who said it or how it was said, the following statements were made to me and a major part of my self-esteem came together. What I heard was:

When people you hold in high regard compliment you or suggest you have done something well and you dismiss or minimize it, you are insulting that person. They would not have said anything they did not find to be true. I had to think about that for a while. I remembered all the times I had done just that, not accepting what they said and, to add insult to injury, I would put myself down. Not a good thing to do. The joy is that I finally 'got it'! Again, this is something I use in my work to help others with finding their self-esteem. It is helpful to be able to say, 'Been there, done that. I DO know what you are going through.'

FOOD FOR THOUGHT

A life lesson that I've learned is that food is remarkably powerful in that it can bring people together in surprising ways that nurture mind, body and soul. A few years ago, my husband

Christine Grantham

and I participated in a social action group in our church called the Latin American Task Force. Although this committee was composed of people from diverse backgrounds, we shared a common interest in the welfare of people living in the developing countries, particularly those of Central and South America. One goal of the Task Force was to raise public awareness of human rights issues in these countries. Another goal was to financially support individuals and non-governmental organizations working to improve circumstances and quality of life in these countries

One vehicle to advance these objectives was an annual fund-raising luncheon, open to all who were interested in learning more about these causes. Various keynote speakers who were advocates and activists

committed to advancing human rights and economic justice in Latin America would report on needs and issues that could be addressed by the group in attendance. Poverty, human rights violations, sweat shop working conditions, and micro-banking are just a few examples of the messages conveyed during these luncheons. The members of the task force prepared a culturally relevant meal for attendees listening to these important messages. I learned that sharing a meal prepared with an abundance of goodwill could bring people together and ultimately benefit those without access to food and the freedom to express their dreams. A favorite of these luncheon recipes follows.

ENSALADA SABROSA RECIPE ON THE NEXT PAGE

ENSALADA SABROSA

INGREDIENTS

1 (15.8 oz) can of cannellini (or navy or white) beans

1 (15.8 oz) can black beans, drained and rinsed

1 1/4 cups pealed and chopped fresh tomatoes

3/4 cup diced sweet red pepper

3/4 cup diced sweet yellow pepper

3/4 cup thinly sliced green onions

1/2 cup salsa

1/4 cup red wine vinegar

2 tablespoons chopped fresh cilantro

1/8 teaspoon freshly ground black pepper

8-10 cups (about 1 head) finely shredded lettuce (romaine works best)

PREPARATION

Combine the cannellini beans, black beans and chopped tomato in a large bowl, stirring gently. Add the red pepper, yellow pepper, and sliced green onion. Stir gently to combine

In a small bowl, combine the salsa, vinegar, cilantro and pepper. Stir with a wire whisk until well blended. Pour the whisked salsa, vinegar, cilantro and pepper over the bean mixture and toss gently. Line a large serving bowl with the shredded lettuce. Top with the bean mixture. Enjoy!

FORGIVENESS

Forgiving is a challenge. When one considers all the books written on the subject, all the sermons preached from the pulpit, and all the "experts" featured on television talk shows, no one escapes the challenge to forgive. I hang on to past hurts and pains that others have inflicted on me. (Did they really hurt me or have I allowed them to do so?) Here's one lesson that was gently brought to my attention a few years ago when I first began working on this book.

Cathy Horvath

I was an excellent student all through my school years, but I was also a nervous wreck. In 5th grade I began to have stomach aches during school. The stomach ache would go away in a few hours, but the next day I would break out in little white blisters under the skin at the tip of my fingers. Those blisters would open up into sores and my hands would really swell up. This was a continuous daily pattern for several months. My parents had a friend who used to give my mother all kinds of home made remedies and advice for everything. She told my folks to soak my hands in bleach to drain the puss from the sores. Well, they used to hold my hands down in the bleach because it was very painful and I would scream. Think about it—open sores in bleach? Not good! Eventually, Mom took me to a doctor who pre-scribed tranquilizers for me and treatments in his office to dry up my skin. It took several weekly office visits, but eventually the skin on my fingertips returned to normal. I think the tranquilizers had a lot to do with calming me down so that the stomach aches and break outs were fewer and far between. I also had a liquid medicine that I had to soak my hands in nightly that turned my hands brown as though I were playing in feces. I wore my dad's fireman's white cotton dress gloves to school. I could hardly hold my pencil—my hands were so swollen. That went on for quite a while. I had problems with the stomach aches and little blisters even into my early adult years, but nothing quite as bad as when I was 10 years old. Whenever I had a particularly stressful experience in high school, dating, planning a wedding, etc. the stomach ache would come, and the blisters followed but I was able to cope on my own and work through the stress.

I relived that memory and many others of punishments and beatings while writing about them. I was a child again and could feel the pain and anguish of those experiences. That was late on a Thursday evening, and tears began to flow as I recounted the events. I stopped writing and went to bed. The "strangest" thing happened two days after writing those memories. My husband and I were shopping in a new store in town. It turned out that the store stocked merchandise primarily for a country style décor so I didn't have much interest. I browsed the shelves nevertheless, thinking I might find some gifts for Christmas. As I turned to my left to keep looking at other displays of merchandise, I had the sudden urge to turn back around to my right to look at the display I had just passed. There on a child's white painted rocker nestled in a corner was a needle pointed pillow that read: *"The greatest gift one can give to another is that of forgiveness."* Well, I had a sudden "knowing" that the pillow had a message meant for me. I thanked my Guardian Angels for reminding me of what I needed to do. Then and there I realized I had to let go of my hurts and painful memories of those childhood experiences. My parents did the best they could. They did not hurt me out of viciousness—they thought they were doing the right thing. They had no other role models. No Oprah, no Dr. Phil, no family magazines to guide their parenting skills. I know they loved me. My challenge was to let go of the pain and hurt—"give it up and over to God." Once in a while the memories return and when they do I tell my parents I forgive them. I move on to a happy memory with them. I don't have to forget —I can't do that. But I can release the emotion and feelings attached to the memory. It's okay now.

FRENCH CREPES

It was Kathy Masters-Jaeckel's dream to move from the Chicago area to Sedona, AZ. She has had her share of very tough times, but always remained focus on her dream. Well, a few years ago she got to her destination via Phoenix where she worked as an esthetician. She

Kathy Masters-Jaeckel

and her husband, Larry, are the proud owners of a magnificent bed and breakfast nestled among the red rocks of Sedona appropriately called Sedona Cathedral Hideaway Bed & Breakfast. They offer their guests a variety of organic dishes from which to choose—not an easy task. What follows is a favorite.

FRENCH CREPES

INGREDIENTS

1 cup milk

1/2 cup flour

2 tablespoon butter

1 teaspoon baking powder

2 eggs beaten

1/2 teaspoon salt

Cinnamon and vanilla or almond extract to taste

PREPARATION

Heat milk and butter in a saucepan. Measure flour by dip-level-pour method. When milk mixture is slightly cooled, pour into a small mixing bowl. Combine dry ingredients and mix together. Slowly whisk dry ingredients into milk and butter. Wisk about 1/3 and then slowly whisk in 1/2 of beaten eggs. Then alternate adding the dry ingredients and the eggs. Let sit in refrigerator for at least an hour. The batter can be refrigerated overnight.

Heat crepe skillet on low until hot. Scoop in about four or five tablespoons of batter and quickly tilt to make batter cover the bottom. Be sure to cover the edges well so they can be flipped easily after about one minute.

When finished pick up pan and flip over on to plate. Serve with fresh fruit.

FRIENDSHIPS

During a recent conversation, my friend lamented over losing touch with an old friend.

Cathy Horvath

"I thought we'd be friends for life. That's what we promised each other when we were growing up. But I haven't heard from her in years. We've sort of lost touch once we moved to other cities and started our families."

I have had the same experience in my life. I learned a valuable life lesson. I used to believe that the friends I had would be my friends forever. After all, we shared our deepest thoughts and feelings at some stage in our lives. We supported each other in troubling times and we shared each other's joys. Why would that ever change?

Simply put, people change. People grow and sometimes people grow apart. I now believe that friends enter our lives for a purpose. When that purpose has been fulfilled, they move on. Friends may appear specifically when we need guidance, comfort or support. Other friends may come to teach us something new, or to help us release something from the past. They may point us in a new direction—one we would never have considered otherwise. When the time is right, these friends move on. It's really okay.

Although some people won't stay friends forever, we can remember them and thank them for being a part of our lives. They brought something to our lives to enrich us and to create a sweet memory. That is a gift to cherish forever.

GARLIC PEPPER STEAK

If I had to choose the most frequently made and most popular recipe in my collection, it would be this one. Everyone I have shared it with through the years has continued to use it and enjoyed kudos from their guests. It's easy, delicious, and is relatively inexpensive when serving several people. This is also a great choice for grilling.

Cathy Horvath

GARLIC
PEPPER
STEAK

INGREDIENTS

1 1/2 - 2 lbs. flank steak

1/4 cup salad oil

2 tablespoons lemon juice

2 tablespoons soy sauce

2 tablespoons chopped green onions or 1 tablespoon dried green onions or minced onions

1 clove garlic crushed
or 1/2 teaspoon garlic powder

1 teaspoon black pepper

1 teaspoon celery salt

PREPARATION

Remove any surface fat from meat. Wipe well with damp towels. In shallow baking dish make marinade by combining all ingredients except meat. Place steak in marinade for 2 hours, turning frequently. Let stand at room temperature. Or leave covered in refrigerator for 6 hours, turning occasionally. Drain marinade from meat and broil the meat 3-4 inches from heat for 3 minutes on each side for rare. Slice in 2 inch pieces on the diagonal.

Serves 6

GERRY'S FUFU and SOUP

Gerry Sides

Although I am an American citizen today, I was born in and grew up in Nimba, Liberia, West Africa. I have many wonderful memories of my childhood there. It was a beautiful area and the people interacted as though they were all members of one large family. Rich memories emerge when I recall my mother cooking my father's favorite meal every Friday. Mother sang as she cooked. When Father got home I ran to hug him; then I watched him eat (in West Africa, the adult man of the house eats alone without the children). Liberia is situated just a few hundred miles north of the equator so the sun sets around 6:00pm all year long. There is very little dusk – just daylight then night. In the evenings, we all sat by the fire and listened to stories told by Father. By the time I was eight years old, I asked Mother if I could cook for Father. To my delight, she said yes. Under her watchful eye, I spent the whole day cooking. When Father got home and was ready to eat, I was so excited and happy that when I served him the food, I spilled most of it. But the little he had, he told me was great. From then on I helped my mother cook every Friday. Cooking with our mothers was the way we Liberian girls learned about and got ready for womanhood.

My father passed away about five years ago, but I keep the tradition going by cooking my family's favorite food every Sunday. The name of the recipe is Fufu and Soup.

FUFU AND SOUP RECIPE ON THE NEXT PAGE

GERRY'S FUFU and SOUP

INGREDIENTS AND PREPARATION:

For the soup you need chicken, beef, onion, green peppers, tomatoes and tomato paste with some hot peppers, and seasonings to taste. Prepare and cook as you would a standard soup recipe.

FuFu is to Western and Central African cooking what mashed potatoes are to American and European cooking. They're made from potatoes and potato starch and formed into a dumpling like mixture. For a simplified method: in a medium size microwaveable bowl, stir together one cup instant mashed potato flakes, 1/2 cup potato starch and about 1/2 cup or more water. Stir until the ingredients are dissolved and mixed well. Set aside for a minute or two to allow the mixture to thicken. Add more water if desired and mix well. (The amount of water used depends upon the consistency desired, remembering that the final outcome is a thick dumpling.)

Place bowl uncovered in a microwave oven for about six minutes on high. Half way through the cooking time, remove bowl and stir to break down any lumps, and return to microwave for the last three minutes. When done, remove bowl and slowly stir the potato mixture until all lumps are thoroughly mashed and the mixture is smooth and elastic. Put water into a small bowl, spoon about 1/3 – 1/2 cup potato mixture into bowl and with wet hands, smooth into a ball.

Place FuFu into an individual serving bowl and cover with soup.

GHANAIAN DOUGHNUT BALLS

John Atiase was among the first students enrolled for the Christian education course I created at the

Reverend Tim Morrison

Evangelical Presbyterian Seminary in Peki, Ghana. He came from the neighboring village of Peki Avetille. In his 50's and having been a middle school leaver, John had not been inside a classroom for over 35 years. During those 35 years he worked as a farmer – tilling the hard Ghanaian soil by hand, growing sufficient crops to feed his family and have some left to sell in the market. John was among the best students in the program.

At the end of the intensive training program, John returned to his village and his church determined to set up a Sunday school program as he had been taught to do at the seminary. He knew the denomination leaders keenly wanted the program to spread rapidly among the congregations of the Evangelical Presbyterian Church of Ghana. John wanted to have the first program.

I kept in touch with John concerning his progress. He brought together a committee. He shared with the committee members everything he had been taught. The committee members liked the idea and understood its merits; however, the program went nowhere. I was perplexed. I knew some of the committee members. They were educated people – several were school teachers, one a university professor emeritus. They understood the power of education. Why was nothing happening?

One afternoon, I walked to Peki Avetille to speak with the pastor. John was a good student; among the best in the class. He understood the concepts and the process. From what I understood, he shared his knowledge with the committee and then the process ground to a halt. Could the pastor help me understand why?

He could and he did: John was a middle school leaver and a farmer. His committee was made up of secondary school completers, college graduates, even one with a PhD. Culture and tradition said that such a common person could not have anything of value to teach the more educated. I had encountered a similar attitude in working with some congregations back in the States.

However, there, in Peki, I had leverage. Not only was I a religious education specialist, I had also been appointed principal of the seminary by the Executives of the church in Ghana. When the next intensive training session began at the seminary with people representing congregations all across Ghana, I brought in John to help teach. He helped teach the making and use of craft projects. He explained how the curriculum was designed to reflect the acute economic crisis in the country – how to use materials on hand rather than scraping scarce currency together to buy paper and pencils and crayons. The students – many of whom were also middle aged with farming backgrounds – responded to John's input.

Two weeks after the close of this training program, John had a Sunday school program up and running in the Peki Avetille church with nearly 200 children in attendance. What had happened? John had taught at the seminary. The principal of the seminary, an education specialist with a doctorate, had turned to John for help in teaching. In all of their collective years as college educated teachers, none of the committee members had ever been invited to teach or to help teach at the seminary. But John had. Apparently he had knowledge worth sharing.

Other villages heard of John's success in Avetille and of his stint at the seminary helping the principal/specialist. Peki Tsame, Peki Afeviefe, Peki Dzake congregations and pastors invited John to help them start their own programs. He went gladly and shared what he had learned and the Sunday school program spread quickly.

TOGBOE (GHANAIAN DOUGHNUT BALLS) RECIPE ON THE NEXT PAGE

Togboe can be served for breakfast or eaten as a midday snack. We asked our cook for the recipe. Selina smiled – this was a culture in which things were passed down orally. One evening as Selina made the dough for the next morning, we measured everything as she went along. For over 30 years, I've been making togboe for my family and sharing the recipe with others.

TOGBOE (GHANAIAN DOUGHNUT BALLS)

INGREDIENTS AND PREPARATION

Combine the following ingredients in a large bowl:

2 cups of water	2 tablespoons of milk or cream
6 tablespoons of sugar	1/4 teaspoon nutmeg
1/4 teaspoon yeast	1 teaspoon salt
1 tablespoon of margarine (butter is acceptable but we did not have butter in the bush village)	

Mix the ingredients by hand preferably with a wooden spoon.

Next add:

4 cups flour - add it slowly and stir/beat with wooden spoon as you add the flour.

Cover and let rise overnight or at least for 5 hours.

Fry tablespoonfuls of dough in hot oil until they are golden brown. The dough balls should turnover in the oil by themselves. If not, turn them so they do not burn.

Togboe is good eaten as it is. However, having a small container of sugar or cinnamon sugar to roll the togboe in adds a delightful and decadent taste.

GUISEPPE SFARA, U.S. CITIZEN

Cathy Horvath

There is a lot of controversy these days over illegal immigration. It's a tough decision for our country's leaders to make and both sides of the argument are, to some degree, valid. However, my thoughts go back to what it took for my grandparents and my husband's grandparents to gain citizenship to this country. Take my paternal Grandfather, for instance. His name was Guiseppe Sfara, born April 8, 1883. He was a native of Cosenza, a large town in the Calabria Region of Italy. When he lost all members of his family to an earthquake that obliterated his home town in 1905, he and a friend signed on to work on the Panama Canal. He was a pipe fitter and earned $.25 an hour to start and then $.50 an hour in gold later on. According to documents I have, he paid a portion of each paycheck to the Isthmian Canal Commission towards transportation to America. Letters of commendation indicate he was a hard worker and an honest man. He survived malaria and yellow fever that took the lives of hundreds of men. He labored there for three years.

Once in America, he married my grandmother, Angelina Fabbri, and settled down to a life of hard work as a pipe fitter for the Pullman Company located on the far south side of Chicago. He walked an average of ten miles a day to and from work, and further on the weekends to St. Anthony Church. He was an usher there for fifty years. He would rise at 5 o'clock on Sunday mornings to get to church to stoke the furnace in order to have heat by the time the first Mass was scheduled. He ran numerous fund raisers for the senior citizen housing in the community and was well known for his philanthropic works. He never stopped working even after officially retiring from his Pullman job. He found a part time job as a janitor at a ladies' boutique near his home. From his meager earnings, each paycheck he would put aside money to the owners so he could buy my mom, aunt, and me a beautiful silk scarf. How I cherished that scarf!

My lesson: a funny one for starters. We used to take long, long walks together when I was a little girl and I would run out of breath trying to keep up with him (today we would say he was a power walker). He would say: "keepa yo moutha shut." He learned that from his Panama Canal days. It helps you from becoming dehydrated.

What I learned from him is his strong work ethic, his dedication to his faith, and his love for his family. He earned his right to become an American citizen—something most of us take for granted. What a man!

GRAND MOM'S COMFORT FOOD

I spent many a Saturday visiting my Grand Mom. She was a lovely lady and very proper. In fact, she reluctantly wore her first pair of slacks at 78 years. Until that time she always wore stockings, a girdle and a slip with her dresses…even in the house with no place to go! She was a gentle woman of routine. On Saturdays for lunch you could expect her delicious, original, melted grilled cheese sandwich with an ice-cold Coca Cola. This was always accompanied by a few dill pickle chips and a big handful of Lay's potato chips.

Pamela Wedding

GRAND MOM'S
ORIGINAL
GRILLED CHEESE
SANDWICH

INGREDIENTS

Grated sharp cheddar cheese

Minced onion

A dash or two of Worchester sauce

PREPARATION

Combine thoroughly. Place between two buttered (on outside) slices of white bread.

Place in an iron skillet or old iron waffle press. Cook until the toast is nicely browned and the cheese oozes out the sides.

Editor's Note: Pamela Wedding says her Grand Mom laughingly called it her 'grilled cheese with a bite'!

GRANDMOTHER IDA'S TORTELLINI

Allan Galassini

This is a recipe handed down from my Grandmother Ida (Fabbri) Galassini. My Mother used it, my generation used it and now the grandchildren use it. Our family tradition continues with making Tortellini for every Christmas dinner. Our family gathers two or three weeks prior to the holiday at a designated family member's residence to make the pasta. Everyone must be there to help including the very young to the eldest. Each has a particular job to do. One person makes the dough and meat filling; another uses the dough machine to roll out the dough. The dough is then passed around the table to be rolled, filled, twisted and set aside. One of the children places the completed tortellini on a tray to be frozen. On Christmas Day we all sit down as a family to eat and enjoy.

GRANDMOTHER IDA'S TORTELLINI RECIPE ON THE NEXT PAGE

GRANDMOTHER IDA'S TORTELLINI

INGREDIENTS AND PREPARATION

3 1/2 lbs. of round steak, veal steak and pork, all ground together once

1 tablespoon olive oil

5-6 eggs

1 1/2 cups bread crumbs

1 lb. grated Asiago cheese

Salt and pepper to taste

Place meat mixture in skillet with 1 tablespoon oil. Do not brown meat—just take the red out. Set aside to cool.

Add to the meat:

5-6 eggs beaten

Bread crumbs

Grated cheese

Salt and pepper to taste

Mix in bread crumbs and small amount of cheese to take the moisture out of the meat. Meat should be easy to handle, but slightly tacky.

Dough:

5 lbs. Sarasota flour

5-6 eggs

Salt and pepper to taste

Lukewarm water

recipe continued on next page

Empty the flour onto a pastry board in a mound. Create a well in the center of the flour mound and add the eggs. Mix the two ingredients together by hand. Add lukewarm water a little at a time and knead well until the dough forms a smooth ball. It is now ready to be rolled out. Once the dough is rolled out in a thin sheet a little less than 1/8 of an inch thick, place the filling the size of a marble on the dough in rows, leaving a small space between each one, and allowing enough dough on one side of the rows to pull over the filling mounds and cover. With a moistened finger or pastry brush, moisten the dough to be covered. As each row is covered, press down with a finger between each mound to define each filling (looks like very small pillows.) Separate by cutting each small mound with a pastry cutter. Take opposite corners to meet each other and twist, pushing the filling up to form a small hat. They are now ready for boiling in broth.

Broth:

1 whole fryer chicken cut in half

1 1/2 lb. beef chuck roast

Parsley

1 whole onion, peeled and quartered

3 stalks celery cut into 2 inch pieces

1 carrot cut into 2 inch pieces

1 clove garlic

Salt and pepper to taste

6 quarts water

Bring the water and salt to a boil in a large stockpot. Place the chicken, beef chuck roast, and the rest of the ingredients in the water and bring it back to a boil, skimming off any foam. Reduce the heat to a simmer, partially cover the pot and cook for 1 1/2 to 2 hours until chicken and meat are tender. Remove the chicken, beef and vegetables and set aside for use another time/recipe. Strain the broth into a large pot, bring to a boil again and add Tortellini. Tortellini are cooked when they rise to the surface of the broth. The tortellini and broth are now ready to serve.

Editor's note: Some Italians serve the tortellini with a sauce. Marinara Sauce is the most popular choice, but they can also be served with grated cheese and olive oil.

GRANDMOTHER MAUDE MANSELL'S DAFFODIL CAKE

Linda Mansell Martin

For almost two years, I served as Events Manager in a one hundred year old farmhouse in Alpharetta, Ga. called The Mansell House. The adjoining garden was the site for many social occasions including special anniversary and birthday parties, weddings, corporate events and meetings. It was a privilege to conduct tours in the vintage property to school groups, tourists, and scouts. As I passed the kitchen and explained how Mrs. Mansell would cook for her large family in the early days, I would mention her famous Daffodil Cake which her descendents fondly remember as being unusual and quite delicious. Linda Mansell Martin, her granddaughter, produced a cookbook of Mansell Family recipes, included in which is the recipe that follows. The book is not available at this time, but Linda graciously allowed me to include the recipe in my collection. I am most honored to present it here.

GRANDMOTHER MAUDE MANSELL'S DAFFODIL CAKE

INGREDIENTS

1 cup cake flour

3/4 cup plus 2 tablespoons sugar

12 egg whites [1 1/2 cups]

1 1/2 teaspoons cream of tartar

1/4 teaspoon salt

3/4 cup sugar

6 egg yolks

1 1/2 teaspoons vanilla

1/2 teaspoon almond extract

CARAMEL ICING

3 cups of sugar, less 3 tablespoons

1/2 cup milk or 1 small can evaporated milk

2 sticks of butter

1 teaspoon vanilla

Pinch of baking soda

recipe continued on next page

PREPARATION OF CAKE:

Blend flour and 3/4 cup plus 2 tablespoons sugar. Set aside.

Measure egg whites, cream of tartar, and salt into a large mixing bowl and beat on a low to medium speed until foamy. Add 3/4 cup of sugar, 2 tablespoons at a time beating at high speed until stiff. In a small bowl beat egg yolks until thick and lemon- colored, about 5 minutes. Fold flavorings into meringue. Then sprinkle the flour-sugar mixture 1/4 at a time over meringue, folding in carefully just until the flour-sugar mixture disappears.

Pour half of the batter into another bowl; gently fold in egg yolks. Pour into 3-8 inch greased pans, making two white and the middle one yellow. Bake at 375 degrees for 40 minutes on the lowest rack until done.

PREPARATION OF ICING:

Put the sugar into a small black iron skillet and cook over high heat. Sir and cook until syrupy. Add to the other ingredients when they start to boil. Start timing for a 3 minute hard boil. Remove from heat and add a pinch of baking soda and vanilla. With an electric mixer, beat until smooth, and creamy. Add a little milk if it gets too thick to spread. Spread on top and sides of cooled cake. (Weather can affect this icing so it is better to make it on a clear day.)

Grandmother Mansell would spread thickened crushed pineapple (cooked with a little water and corn starch) between the layers of Daffodil Cake with the caramel icing on the sides and top. She kept this cake stored in a cool room. Delicious!

FOR BUSY WIVES:

Buy an angel food cake mix and make according to package directions. Color 1/3 batter yellow and pour into one of three 8″ cake pans. Almost as good as if made from scratch.

GRANDPA'S FIREHOUSE VEGETABLE SOUP

Cathy Horvath

While a Chicago fireman, my Dad had to take turns in the kitchen preparing a hearty meal for the group. He came up with a soup that he called "Grandpa's Firehouse Vegetable Soup." He was quite proud of his creation and made it for all the members of the family whenever we came to visit. After he retired, unbeknown to him, I submitted his recipe for inclusion in a cookbook that the Marshall Field's Department Store in Chicago published as a fund raiser in 1995. At that time, "Field's" was a member of the Dayton's and Hudson's family of stores. In 1989 a tradition began with the publication of a cookbook containing contributions from customers and employees, as well as recipes from the stores' own kitchens. Net proceeds each year were donated to local United Way agencies.

When his recipe was accepted and published, I sent him a copy as a surprise. The day it was scheduled to be delivered, I called my folks in Mountain Home, AR. where they retired and asked them not to leave the house—that a special package was going to arrive. "Give me a quick call to let me know when you get it," I said. So I anxiously waited by the phone in my office for a call, even skipping lunch so I wouldn't miss their call. Hours went by—no call. I drove home from work wondering what could have happened. Did the book not arrive? Did they have a medical emergency that took them away from home? (I hope they're OK.) Shortly after I arrived home, my Mom called to say that the book had just arrived. I had inserted a note that simply read "Surprise!" on the recipe's page. According to Mom, surprised he was, a little astonished, and just a little teary eyed too. My family, friends, and co-workers and I bought several copies of the cookbook. When the family gathered for Christmas at my house that same year, he sat down at the dining room table and autographed each one personally, just like a big literary star.

Here's that special recipe:

GRANDPA'S FIREHOUSE VEGETABLE SOUP RECIPE ON THE NEXT PAGE

GRANDPA'S FIREHOUSE VEGETABLE SOUP

INGREDIENTS

1 lb. lean ground beef

1 gallon water

1 medium onion, diced

1/2 cup lentils

3 celery ribs, diced

1/2 cup pearl barley

2 cloves garlic, minced

1/2 cup chopped fresh parsley

1 26 oz. can chili beans, undrained

salt and pepper to taste

1 16 oz. can kidney beans, drained

3 bay leaves

1 16 oz. can diced tomatoes, undrained

2 medium potatoes cut into 1/2 inch cubes

1 8 oz. can tomato sauce

1 1/2 cups small pasta shells

PREPARATION:

In a large pot, combine beef, onion, celery and garlic. Cook over medium heat until beef is no longer pink. (8-10 minutes).

Stir in chili beans, kidney beans, tomatoes, tomato sauce, water, lentils, barley, parsley, salt, pepper and bay leaves. Increase heat to medium-high and bring mixture to a boil. Reduce heat to medium-low and cook, uncovered, until barley is almost cooked (35-40 minutes).

Add potatoes, pasta, and, if soup is too thick, additional water. Cook until potatoes and pasta are tender (10-15 minute) and serve. Cook longer for a stew-like consistency.

Serves 12-16

GRIEF IS NOT JUST ABOUT DEATH

Cathy Horvath

My youngest sister, Christine, has been involved in the Hospice field for several years. During our weekly conversations (she lives in Pennsylvania and I live in Georgia) she relates her experiences with death and dying, and the impact not only on the patient, but the extended family as well. She recently attended a multi-day seminar on the dying process and, at my request, sent me a couple of books to read. The books got me to thinking about loss and grief.

According to a 2001 survey conducted by researcher Anne Spurgeon and colleagues, death of a spouse or loved one is the number one stressor in a person's life. It is followed by a divorce or break-up of a relationship, a job loss, retirement, illness and many other losses. We suffer losses throughout the course of a lifetime. When we were kids our favorite pet passed away. Perhaps our best friend since kindergarten moved to a new city. As we got older, our grandparents may have passed away. When my grandson was away at college he learned that his best friend since grammar school had been killed in an auto accident and around the same time, my grandson's dog of 17 years died. Fast forward to current times and what are the most troublesome life issues we are dealing with today? Loss of a job held for many years accompanied by loss of an income and self identity, the loss of a marriage through divorce, bankruptcy, losing a home to foreclosure, aging...the list goes on and on.

Most of us have experienced loss. Until a few years ago, I never realized that my sadness and depression over the loss of a job I really enjoyed were really grief. I always attributed grieving to someone dying whom we loved and missed. After a long conversation, a friend pointed out that what I was experiencing was grief. That stopped me in my tracks! I thought about it. She was right! She also pointed out that spending so much time grieving prevented me from taking the steps necessary to move forward to what she called "the next adventure in my life." That made a lot of sense to me.

Since that conversation, I have lost both my parents, my dear aunts and uncles, a close cousin, another job, and moved from my city of birth and former home of 30 years to a new home in a new city. I understand the grieving process better now and allow a finite period of time to recover. I am not proposing any particular process for everyone for we are each individuals who react to life in our own unique way. What I do suggest is that when you experience a job loss, foreclosure, bankruptcy, or any other loss, that grief is natural. But you can and should reach out for ways to recover from grief. Buy a book on the subject, attend a seminar, talk to your minister or rabbi, search the web—do something to help yourself move forward. It will not only benefit you, but it will impact your family and friends as well.

GRISSINI (Bread Sticks)

Dolly Galassini's son, Allan, has taken great care to keep the recipes his mother used and carry on her cooking traditions. His close knit family continues to create her dishes, particularly during the holidays. I give him and his siblings a lot of credit for doing so.

Allan Galassini

GRISSINI
(BREAD STICKS)

INGREDIENTS

3 cups flour

1 teaspoon salt

1 stick butter (1/2 cup) at room temperature

1 package dry yeast

1 teaspoon sugar

1 cup warm water

PREPARATION

Mix sugar with 1 cup warm water. Add yeast. Let stand until yeast is dissolved.

Mix flour and salt; cut butter into flour (as with pie dough) then add yeast to flour, mixing well. (I use mixer with dough hook if you have one.) Turn out on floured board or canvas and knead for 12-15 minutes, adding flour as necessary to get a smooth, stiff dough.

Place in a greased bowl. Cover and place in a warm place until double in size, about 1 1/2 hours. Turn out of bowl. Let rest 15 minutes.

Take thumb size pieces and roll out with fingers and palm of hands to length of a cookie sheet. Shorter if you prefer.

Place on ungreased cookie sheet, cover and let rest about 15 minutes. Bake 25-30 minutes until lightly brown at 350 degrees. Makes about 3 cookie sheets or about 1 pound of sticks.

*You can use garlic salt to add to the taste. Good eating!

HARD TIMES CHILI

Richard Morgan, a dear friend for many years, shares this memorable recipe: "During the Great Depression, my Uncle Manuel Theodore made and sold this chili to restaurants. He was able to support our extended family of 16, living together in St. Louis in one big house on Plymouth Avenue. He was employed by the St. Louis Grand Opera building and designed stage settings. The story goes that he was able to obtain our grand house through his connections with the Opera."

Richard Morgan

HARD TIMES CHILI

INGREDIENTS

3 lbs boneless chuck, diced in 1/2 inch cubes

1/4 lb hard suet (beef or pork)diced; reserve cracklings

2 oz. bottle McCormick chili powder (or Gebhardt's brand)

2 oz. bottle McCormick paprika

1 oz. ancho chili powder

6 cloves garlic, minced

1/2 cup all purpose flour

1/2 cup Masa Harina (Mexican corn flour)

Salt

Pepper

2 tablespoons McCormick comino seeds, toasted and ground

1 teaspoon McCormick oregano leaves, or to taste

2 cans pinto beans (optional)

Small onion, diced (optional)

1-6 oz can tomato sauce (optional)

recipe continued on next page

PREPARATION:

Put suet in heavy bottomed pot and render on medium-high heat.

Place 1/3 of the chuck and brown it off in the pot. Remove meat from pot.

Brown off second 1/3 of chuck. Remove it from pot.

Brown remaining 1/3 chuck. Return browned meat to pot.

(Add onions now, if using.)

Add minced garlic and chili powders, paprika, and comino seeds.

(Add tomato paste now, if using.)

When thoroughly mixed add 3 cups hot water, and reduce heat to simmer.

Add oregano.

Simmer until meat is tender, adding more water as needed to obtain desired consistency.

Make a slurry of flour, Masa Harina and cold water and add to pot, stirring until blended.

Simmer another 20 minutes.

Add rinsed pinto beans (if using) and heat thoroughly.

Serve with sides of condiments listed, perhaps adding diced tomatoes.

MAY BE SERVED WITH:

1 bag grated cheddar cheese

Jalapenos (canned slices)

1 pint container sour cream (not non-fat)

Frito Lay corn chips

Bunch fresh cilantro

HOMAGE TO MISS EMMA

Stan W. Darden

Her name was Emma Turner, but all her co-workers at the Krystal Restaurant in Decatur, GA, called her simply "Miss Emma," and they spoke it with the deepest respect. She had managed the restaurant for several years. The upper management of the Tennessee-based Krystal was well aware of her leadership skills, but I wonder if they ever knew of her other skills: providing succor and healing to anyone whose life touched hers in that tiny but teeming orbit of a bustling and successful restaurant.

Did I neglect to mention? She saved my life as I struggled to recover from the end of my 20-year marriage, three bankruptcies (two corporate filed by United Press International where I had been employed, one personal) and a loss of self-worth that accompanied those tribulations. For you see, to me Miss Emma was an angel in the form of a beautiful black woman with the sole purpose of recovering the lost and restoring sanity to the lives of people who had nearly lost theirs. I may not be religious in the conventional sense of the term, but I know an angel when I meet one.

After the UPI debacle, I was trying to eke out a living as a freelance journalist in the mid-1990s, when it became painfully obvious that I was not going to survive with the pitiful amount of work I was doing for a small North Georgia newspaper and a couple of Atlanta magazines. So I called a friend who was an executive with Krystal. He arranged for me to land a job as a management trainee with the restaurant chain. Some management trainee! A man in his mid-50s looking like a modern version of Willie Loman, the anti-hero of Arthur Miller's epic play *Death of a Salesman*.

My first day on the job I was given my uniform, a snazzy button down blue Oxford cloth shirt with pants and — the finishing touch — a jaunty baseball cap with Krystal printed on it. Looking at myself in the mirror, I thought, "So here's the guy who used to work on the World News Desk of United Press International, one of the world's premier news wire services. What a fall from grace! What could be more embarrassing?" That was the self-pitying side of me, nearly a full-time job in those days.

I was given training in preparing Krystals, little burgers that were very delicious, with just the right amount of onion taste. All my co-workers pitched in to make sure I was learning the right way to do my job. "Hey," I said, "this isn't such a bad gig after all. I might even grow to like it."

Presiding over all my training, as she did over the entire operation of the restaurant was Miss Emma, the undisputed boss of the place. She was a regal looking woman who stood above average height and carried herself with great dignity in her bearing. She was imposing physically and she gave the impression that she wasn't about to take any crap from anyone. But the most obvious character trait of all — at least to me — was the almost palpable sense of empathy and caring for her employees and customers, who adored her.

When I had been there about two weeks, she came to me and said, "I've been watching you and I can see you're not a weak man. As a matter of fact, you're a strong man who knows a lot about life. What you don't know we'll teach you here." And that's what she proceeded to do over the course of the year I spent working under her leadership. A recurring phrase I heard in connection with her was, "Miss Emma could run General Motors if she had more formal education."

I stuck with Krystal long past the time when we gave up the fiction that I was a management trainee, which was a ruse to give me a financial boost in life. But there was far more than money involved in what transpired between Miss Emma and me. She set me on the road to recovery of my life and dignity. She stomped the self-pity out of me and replaced it with the love of God and my fellow humankind. She was my guardian-protector and I loved her.

Shortly before I left Krystal to re-enter the journalism field and marry my wife, Miss Emma said to me, "You know, some day you're going to write something about me." Once again, Miss Emma was right. This is that "something." That was many years ago, but I believe Miss Emma knows that I have written about her. I believe, too, that she knows she has a special place in my heart and that I cherish her memory.

HONESTY AMIDST FRUSTRATION

Cathy Horvath

Recruited by my employer to generate more and new revenue for the company's relocation division, I took on the challenge with high energy and positive intention. I inherited a small but competent staff. Working closely with them, I began to achieve success. Business volume began to increase substantially. It became apparent we needed additional staff. I was given authorization by the CEO to begin interviewing people for a few positions. Creating advertisements, screening candidates, and interviewing them are arduous tasks and quite time consuming. More time consuming than you can imagine.

I finally narrowed the search down to a few prospects and made my selection. One particular candidate came well prepared. She had a good resume that reflected just the right experience and skills for the job. The interview went well. I told her I would require senior management's approval to move forward. Well, that never happened. What I wasn't told was that there was a hiring freeze during the time I was selecting candidates. No explanation—I just couldn't extend an offer to this person. She called several times and it became very difficult to put her off any longer without an honest explanation. I wasn't given any so I couldn't give her one. I finally told her the truth and suggested that she continue to seek employment. If a job came along that was a good match for her, I suggested she take it. I apologized and offered my help in any way. She was most appreciative for my honesty. I never heard from her again.

Fast forward about 6 years. I took a position as an Account Executive for a firm that offered a service to the relocation industry. I covered the entire nation and called upon personnel at the director level. I usually began my sales process over the phone by introducing myself and explaining the menu of services my company offered. I did so to the Director for a Corporate Relocation Company in Arizona. The words were rolling smoothly off my tongue when the prospect interrupted me and said "Your name is Cathy Horvath? Weren't you Vice President for such and such company in Chicago?" When I responded affirmatively, she said, much to my amazement: "I'm Cheryl so and so. I interviewed for a job with you. You were so honest with me I never forgot you. What are you doing now? Whatever it is, I'm interested. Tell me more."

Wow! I ended up signing that company as a new client. She trusted that what I said I could do, I would deliver. Being honest and living with integrity in your day-to-day business activities are vital components to success, no matter what your endeavors. You just never know. I could have blown her off when she called so often about that job, but I just couldn't do that. I treated her as I would want to be treated.

By the way, the reason for the freeze on hiring so suddenly was that the company was put up for sale. Wish I had known that up front—it would have saved a lot of time and effort!

HOT APPLE CIDER

Cathy Horvath

I have lived most of my life in the Chicago area. As Oprah once commented, Chicagoans experience nine months of winter each year. When you've lived there long enough, you get used to it, I guess. Our home of twenty nine years was situated on an acre and a half of land in a semi-rural suburban area. Most of the lot backed up to a buffer area to a Forest Preserve that surrounded Argonne National Laboratories. One of my favorite winter afternoon treats occurred after a heavy snowfall when everything in the back yard was coated in glistening white snow. As I sat at my kitchen table looking out the bay window I could easily spot a bright red cardinal or two perched on a snow covered tree limb. What a sight! I had the pleasure of enjoying a holiday greeting card come to life. Part of this magical experience was sipping on a mug of hot apple cider. Not just any cider, mind you. I did my best to replicate one that was served in a restaurant that was a standard luncheon spot for a ladies' day out. Sip it slowly, relax, and enjoy the experience. Winter won't seem so bad after all!

RECIPE:

Brew apple cider and add cinnamon or peppermint schnapps to taste. Pour into large mug and garnish with a cinnamon stick and lemon slice.

HUMILITY AND CIRCUMSTANCE

While in high school, I worked during the summers in a printing company that was managed by my father. On blistering-hot, summer days, the strong stench of ink and paper made the air in the plant more stifling. While my father was the boss, I worked in the factory area where printed sheets were cut and then folded and stapled into glossy advertising booklets or direct mail pieces. Many times, these were brochures for the new fall lineup of cars. I enjoyed being one of the first to see the newest version of the 1971 Chevy Camaro or Dodge Charger.

During these summers I learned many lessons about hard work and humility. Most of the people who worked on the factory floor were uneducated, and many were single mothers who were supporting children (sometimes 3 or 4) by working two or more jobs. Each of these jobs required some level of repetitious physical activity. Some people were "board loaders" – loading large sheets of freshly printed paper onto machines that would fold them into booklets. Other people would be stationed at the opposite end of these large machines and took the folded booklets and placed them into boxes for shipping. As if the summer heat wasn't enough, the machines themselves generated considerable noise and heat – making for long, tiring, monotonous days. In addition, the paper stock used for these booklets was glossy and sharp, and would irritate or cut the ends of your fingers as you handled the paper, adding one more element to the discomfort of the job.

During each eight-hour shift, we would get two 15 minute breaks and a half-hour lunch break. Loud buzzers that sounded throughout the factory signaled the start of these break times. How individuals used these 15 minute breaks gave me a better understanding of hard work. For some of the women who worked multiple jobs, these breaks were used as their sleeping time. The buzzer would go off and they would drop their heads and catch a few winks. When the buzzer re-sounded, they woke up and started to work again. Coming from the world as the boss' son, I was amazed at how these people lived and worked. Even more amazing was the gentle spirit and positive attitude of many of these women. While these machines cranked, some sang gospel tunes or just hummed the melodies. I was awestruck at the ability of some of these people to go from one difficult job to the next, singing along the way while knowing that many of my friends would never consider working in that environment, much less working two jobs like this.

The simplicity of their lives, their

humility in accepting difficult conditions and feeling glad that they had the privilege of work have stayed with me all of my life. To this day, I have an admiration for those who work long hours for little pay, often times in jobs that serve those who are fortunate enough to be blessed with better circumstances. I don't have the back for landscape work or the feet for being a waiter –and I suppose neither do many of the people who do those jobs. Our recent economy has shown that circumstances can change in a nanosecond and any one of us could be working in jobs such as these. I wonder how each of us would approach those circumstance? It's something to pay attention to and a life lesson worth learning.

Editor's note: the author of this lesson prefers to remain anonymous. That is his prerogative.

I WAS WRONG!

When I became a member of the senior management team in a large company in downtown Chicago, I was included in weekly meetings with the General Manager and Regional Vice Presidents.

Cathy Horvath

New to the high level corporate environment, I was eager to learn all I could from their experiences and opinions. One comment in particular struck me as odd, but I took it at face value, nevertheless, since its source was a highly regarded executive. "Never admit you made a mistake or you weaken your position with the people who report to you or with whom you interact." When an occasion arose where that comment could have been put to use, I just couldn't do it. I decided to follow my own instincts. (Most of the time we're better off doing that anyway.) The result was that a potentially serious situation was resolved to the mutual satisfaction of both parties, myself included. I felt good about the outcome, especially that I have been honest in my dealings.

So here's the lesson I learned: Don't be afraid to admit you're wrong, whether to a spouse, a child, a friend or a client, etc. You will be respected and appreciated if all you say is "I'm sorry. I made a mistake." Or, "I'm terribly sorry there has obviously been a breakdown in communication", or simply "I screwed up." Say whatever you need and want to say. I'm sure you get the drift. Follow up by saying something like "How can I fix things?" Or, "What can I do to make amends?" It works, it really does! Time and time again I have observed others follow the same advice and have salvaged huge business accounts, a marriage, or important relationships.

IF YOUR JOB DEFINES YOU…

Cathy Horvath

If your job defines you, create another you. That sounds simple enough, doesn't it? Not really. Creation takes determination and hard work. These days thousands of people are without employment—many thinking it would never happen to them. Some planned for it, like retirees. Either way, unemployment comes with a lot of issues—financial, social, and emotional. Whether you've been fired, laid off or retired, most of the struggles are the same.

We have spent the better part of our adult lives adhering to a schedule. Our day is controlled by the clock. Got to get up by a certain time, eat breakfast and get on the road by a certain time or make a 7 a.m. train. Then there's the work schedule—whether you are a white or blue collar worker you are controlled by a schedule. Meetings, routes, plane flights, all at a specific time of day. Come home from work, pick up the kids at school, take them to the dentist or doctor at a specified time, drive the others to piano or soccer practice, drive home, make dinner, help with homework, get the kids to bed—all by a certain hour of the day. Men's days may be a bit different depending on their circumstances but we are all pretty much slaves to the clock. What then, do you do when you wake up in the morning and there is no schedule for your day? No train to catch or time to get on the road because you have no job. You're laid off or you're retired. What's worse is that you no longer have a title or a job description. You are no longer delivery man, service technician, nurse, billing clerk, regional director, sales manager, CEO, vice president, etc. You identified with your title or job and your title or job defined who you are and how others saw you. What do you do now?

Some say it's a good time to reflect on your life and your achievements, the skills you've developed, and your passion. There's the operative word: Passion. All too often we stuck with a job that was unfulfilling because it paid the bills and we enjoyed the perks the paychecks provided. Now is the time to re-evaluate what makes you sing. What is your passion?

Since my retirement, I have met several folks who have redefined who they are and found their passion. One man always enjoyed gardening even though there was never enough time to do all that he wanted. Now he is a Master Gardener and has a small business designing and planting beautiful gardens. He is so good at it because gardening is his passion. Through word of mouth he is enjoying a blossoming (forgive the pun) business. I always enjoyed writing—speeches, press releases, policy and procedures, training manuals, etc. so I wrote this book. A friend who is formerly an Emergency Room nurse who always had an interest in alternative medicine is now a holistic practitioner and nutritionist. Another man who was a former high school history teacher is now a consultant to local historical societies and is quite respected in the community. History is his passion. A neighbor of his is a retired controller who, too, enjoyed learning about the history of his town from the local townsfolk who were getting up in years. Their tales of life growing up in the South during and after the Depression fascinated him and so, in honor of the town's Sesquicentennial Celebration, collaborated on a book containing stories and photos of the old town, its schools, churches, and residents.

My husband took classes in stained glass and set up a workshop upon retiring after 40 years at a corporate job he merely tolerated. He now appears at art fairs and enjoys the positive feedback he receives for his work. A lady I reconnected with just a few weeks ago shared her excitement over graduating in six weeks from a world renowned culinary school. A fifteen year executive of a mortgage brokerage firm, she was unexpectedly laid off without any prior notice or package. Nothing. Her real passion

was cooking; so much so that she catered on weekends. As part of her curriculum she is interning with a company that does food research and creates healthy and interesting menus for restaurants, nursing homes and hospitals. She hopes to join the firm on a permanent basis. When she talks about her current endeavor, her eyes sparkle and her face lights up. She has found her path.

Are you getting any inspiration from all this? I sure hope so. I had a really tough time adjusting to life after corporate but it's been worth the journey through self exploration and appreciation for the accomplishments I've had. When I interviewed for the last part-time job I had, I was asked if I were retired. Now, I know I shouldn't have been asked that question, but I proudly responded "Yes, according to society, I am considered retired. But my body, mind and spirit are far from it." I got the job and spent a wonderful two years as an Events Manager for a vintage property. A complete departure from my corporate days but I utilized those skills I learned, cofounded an organization of wedding industry service providers, planned expos, and just relished each day I was a part of a totally new life.

IT ALL STARTED WITH A LIBRARY BOOK

Cathy Horvath

As I mentioned in the Introduction to this book, I have always been a "Martha Stewart wanna be." When I was about 8 years old, Martha Stewart was not yet "Martha Stewart." I shadowed my mother every night as she prepared dinner. When she cleaned up the pots and pans she used to prepare the meal, she let me add the potato peelings, onion bits, and anything else I could scrape together from the preparations into a large pan. I would add, stir and mix—pretending I was instructing an audience. Then a wonderful thing happened—my school library got in a brand new cook book for beginners! I checked it out, returned it when it was due, then checked it out again. This went on for several months until the Librarian called my mother and suggested she purchase the book for me; which she did. The name of the book was *"Fun With Cooking…Easy Recipes for Beginners"* by Mae Blacker Freeman. It cost a whopping $1.50 but I sure got my mother's money's worth out of it. I still have it to this day. (The book was reprinted in 1973 and is available used from Amazon.com.) As you skimmed the pages of my cook book, when you came to page 24, you would find a heavily soiled, well used page. It featured the recipe for French Toast. Then there's page 26 which featured Hamburger Patties. But the messiest page of all features

Peanut Butter Cookies. I made them quite often. Another favorite recipe was for Butterscotch Squares. About the time I was 10 years old, I prepared complete chicken dinners for the family. Cooking and baking were my hobbies; I really wasn't all that interested in paper dolls or baseball.

When my children were growing up, I encouraged them to watch me or to be near the kitchen as I prepared meals. As each of my children turned 4 years of age, we would make Jell-O together. Next we mastered the art of baked potatoes. Then cookies. As they grew older, I guided them in preparing complete meals (hamburgers, chicken, sloppy joes, etc.). All four children are adults now, but each of them (2 men and 2 women) knows their way around a kitchen—and as Martha Stewart would say "That's a good thing."

BUTTERSCOTCH SQUARES RECIPE ON THE NEXT PAGE

BUTTERSCOTCH SQUARES

INGREDIENTS

1/4 cup butter

1 cup brown sugar

1 egg

1 teaspoon vanilla

1/2 cup flour

1 teaspoon baking powder

1/2 teaspoon salt

1/2 cup chopped nutmeats

PREPARATION

Melt the butter in a saucepan over a small flame. Add the brown sugar and stir until dissolved. Remove from the flame and when the mixture has cooled a little, put in the egg, beating until smooth. Then stir in the vanilla. Put a piece of waxed paper on the table and onto it sift, all together, the flour, baking powder and salt. Now carefully lift the waxed paper in one hand and pour the flour slowly into the saucepan mixture, stirring all the while with the other hand. When the mixture is well blended, add the nutmeats.

Next cut the waxed paper to fit the bottom of a pan about 8 by 8 inches. Pour the mixture in, spreading it evenly with the back of a spoon. Bake in a medium oven, 350 degrees, for 30 minutes. As soon as you remove it from the oven, cut into squares, taking out each square separately. Be wary of the hot pan!

ITALIAN NUT COOKIES

Gloria Pascente is the bravest, strongest, determined woman I have had the privilege of knowing. Those words might suggest she is stubborn and she is—in a good way. Her "stubbornness" helped her survive a very serious bout with cancer. She has been through many a challenge in her life but I am sure she would agree that her cancer battle was the toughest. She remains a healthy and loving wife, mother and grandmother today. She is a treasured friend and I wish we could be together more often than my yearly trip to the Southwest where she currently resides. This is the recipe I requested that she contribute:

Gloria Pascente

"My mom died ten years ago and I have been asking all the relatives if they had a copy of this recipe. Every one enjoyed the cookie but no one had the recipe. Recently I was going through a recipe box that was my mother-in-law's and she had this recipe plus my mom's cheese cake recipe. I have come close to duplicating many of mom's recipes just from memory, but I could never quite get this one correct. Mom wrote down many of her recipes but most were in her head."

ITALIAN NUT COOKIES

INGREDIENTS COOKIES

1 cup granulated sugar

2 cups sifted all purpose flour

1 cup butter or margarine.

2 teaspoons vanilla extract

1/4 teaspoon almond extract

1/2 teaspoon salt

1 cup chopped walnuts

INGREDIENTS FROSTING

1 1/2 cups sifted powdered sugar

1/4 cup butter

1/2 teaspoon almond extract

milk

PREPARATION

Combine all ingredients into one bowl and mix with hands until dough is smooth and well blended. Shape into balls the size of a walnut and place about 2 inches apart on an ungreased cookie sheet. Flatten each cookie lightly with a fork (you will see light imprint of fork tines.) Bake at 325 degrees for about 25 minutes or until delicate brown. Cool and frost.

PREPARATION OF FROSTING

Cream butter, sugar, and almond extract. Add just enough milk to make the frosting spreadable then frost cookies.

95

ITALIAN SAUSAGE SANDWICH

One evening my dad joined my husband and children for an informal supper. Mom was already in Arkansas getting their retirement home ready. Not one to give compliments so easily, Dad praised the sandwich by saying something like: "Now this is what I call a real Italian Sausage Sandwich." Then he quickly followed up with "So where did you get the recipe?" He was a bit taken aback when I told him I made it up!

Cathy Horvath

ITALIAN
SAUSAGE
SANDWICH

INGREDIENTS

1 to 1 1/2 lbs. Italian sausage, mild, sweet or hot

2 8 ounce cans tomato sauce

1 green pepper chopped

2 medium onions chopped

1 small can mushroom pieces

1 tablespoon Italian herbs

1 clove garlic

olive oil

shredded Mozzarella cheese

PREPARATION

Grill the sausage links. While they're cooking, fry the green pepper, onions, mushrooms and garlic in a small amount of olive oil. Add the Italian herbs and simmer for 1/2 hour. Place sausage on 6 inch French bread roll, cover with sauce and sprinkle with shredded mozzarella cheese.

Can be served without bun as an entrée with fettuccine noodles and pesto sauce as a side.

IT'S NOT MY FAULT

When I was a boy, my older brother and I were mortal enemies. He was two years older than me, just big enough and strong enough to end every one of our fights with me in a headlock, or pinned on the floor, or stuffed behind the couch.

Dean Grantham

So I did what any normal kid would do – I perfected techniques to get him into so much trouble that he was constantly under attack by my personal bodyguards: our parents. A simple, effective tactic was to bait him with a sneer, which would prompt him to lunge at me. If I were lucky, as he tackled me, we'd bump into a table, tipping over a lamp. By the time my enforcers arrived I'd be whimpering on the floor with him sitting on my chest. As our parents pulled us apart I'd whine, "He started it – it's not *my* fault!" Eventually of course, our parents wised up. But, what about me? Am I still falling for that line?

"It's not my fault." Of course, it's true my words and actions are interwoven with the words and actions of others, so it's not always easy to draw a straight line between cause and effect. Sometimes things just happen. Feelings get hurt. Lives go in unfortunate directions. But, how many things that happen in and around my life are my fault – and I simply don't recognize it?

Consider the example of a physician who lived in Vienna in the 1840's. Back then, medicine was very different than now – the existence of bacteria and viruses was unknown, and medicine focused on treating one's symptoms. Inflammation meant you had too much blood, so leeches were applied to your skin. Difficulty breathing meant you needed better ventilation, so some windows were opened. The physician, Ignatz Semmelweis, was in charge of two maternity wards at Vienna General Hospital. In one, the mortality rate for new mothers was about one in fifty, a very high mortality rate by modern standards. In the other ward though, it was dreadfully worse: one in eight. Time and time again, mothers fell ill and died from symptoms that became known as child-bed fever. But the cause was unknown.

Semmelweis wanted to figure out why one ward was so much more deadly than the other. Well, there was one obvious difference between the two wards: midwives were the caregivers in the ward with the lower mortality, while the caregivers in the ward with the high mortality were doctors, including Semmelweis himself. But Semmelweis couldn't imagine that he and his doctors had anything to do with the problem, so he looked at every other possible alternative. He standardized everything from birthing procedures to food – he even standardized how the laundry was washed, yet the discrepancy between the wards remained. Finally, only after eliminating all other possibilities, Semmelweis was forced to consider whether it might just have something to do with him, and his doctors. Vienna General was a teaching hospital, and the doctors were doing autopsies and research on cadavers. Semmelweis developed a theory that some sort of deadly "particles" were being transferred from the cadavers to the patients, on the hands of the physicians.

He instituted a program of hand-washing in a solution of chlorine and lime, and immediately the mortality rate of the deadly ward dropped to the rate of the other one.

Later in life Semmelweis, unable to forgive himself for the length of time it took him to recognize – literally – his own hand in the spread of child-bed fever, was haunted by the thought of how many people went to their graves prematurely.

So now I have to ask, what particles are on *my* hands? What particles are embedded in my personality, embedded in my habitual ways of responding to stress, embedded in my emotional baggage, that keep me from being a better spouse, a better parent, a better friend, a better citizen in my community? What things do I do, what words do I use, what facial expressions do I display, what inflections of attitude do I add to my voice that kills the initiative and enthusiasm of my coworkers, that damages the self-esteem of my children, or my students, or so many others with whom I come into contact every day?

And what about those actions I *fail* to take, those words I *fail* to say, that might have meant for someone the difference between hope and despair, the difference between pride and shame? Those particles of - inaction - may be on my hands as well.

"It's not my fault."

When we were kids, those words, right or wrong, were a common refrain. As "responsible" adults we almost never say them out loud. But if we unconsciously employ those unspoken words to avoid taking responsibility for our own hidden fears, our own hidden frustrations, then the very things we suffer from will be transmitted to those whose lives we touch.

And whose fault is that?

J.J.'S AWESOME APPLE CAKE

Ever since he was a toddler, our grandson J.J., has enjoyed cooking and baking in my kitchen. He especially liked to make sugar cookies and would carefully measure the rolled out dough to be certain it was precisely 1/4 inch thick. (That was sort of my doing since I wanted all the cookies to cook evenly.) As he grew older, so did the complexities of the recipes we would make together. He has since "graduated" to Biscotti, Ravioli and Chicken Paprikash which he learned from my husband Ray. He called me last year to announce he was designing and opening up a pizza parlor for his friend. The best part of the announcement was that he had created his own recipes for crust and toppings. That's my boy!

J.J. Horvath

In September of 1998 he proudly shared this Apple Cake recipe which he created in his Middle School Home Economics class. I must say, it is the simplest recipe I have ever made and is quite delicious. To this day, whenever I have a few apples left over, I whip out this recipe. It's great for brunch, or served warm with Vanilla Ice Cream. Just typing this anecdote makes me want to walk to my kitchen and make it. It doesn't take much time at all—that's <u>the beauty of it</u>!

J.J.'S AWESOME APPLE CAKE RECIPE ON THE NEXT PAGE

J.J.'S
AWESOME
APPLE CAKE

INGREDIENTS

4 to 5 apples

2 teaspoons cinnamon

3/4 cup oil

4 eggs

1 1/4 cups sugar

1 tablespoon baking powder

2 cups flour

PREPARATION:

Preheat oven to 350 degrees.

Grease and flour 13x9x2 pan.

Peel, core and slice the apples; put them in a large bowl and sprinkle with cinnamon.

In a medium bowl mix oil, eggs and sugar. Mix together the baking powder and flour and add to the oil, eggs and sugar mixture. Blend until combined.

Pour batter over apples and stir until apples are just coated.

Pour into the pan and bake for 35 to 45 minutes.

JACKIE GOLDSTEIN'S GOAL SETTING

I had just started my job as the Art Director of Turner Broadcasting and was invited to speak to a group of college art students. One asked me what was the most important thing that I had done to attain such a great achievement.

Jackie Goldstein, Creative Alchemist

I answered that the most important thing that I had done was to set very specific goals and then work towards them. My goals had been to: become an Art Director of a substantial agency or organization, to win a national design award, to make a specific salary... all before I was 30. Everyone looked at me waiting to hear..., "And as you know I'm Art Director of Turner Broadcasting, I have won numerous national and international awards, I am making that salary... and next month I turn 30!" Yep. I got a big ovation for that one. It was actually the first time that I had taken stock of my accomplishments and goals like that.

I think that sometimes the hardest thing is to set a goal; not because we think too big, but because we don't think big enough. Once you start to think bigger you see your goals in stages and suddenly they are not so impossible. Recently I set new goals for myself. They seemed really ambitious.

I told them to people and refined them so they would become more real to me. After awhile my goals felt so real that they didn't really seem like goals, but like things that had already happened. Having experienced so many successes, my goals are much bigger now. I have started to share them with a few people and have actually found people who can help me put them in motion.

It is very important to share your goals with others. People do want to help you reach your goals and they want to feel like they contributed to your success. Align yourself with people who will be proud to see you succeed. Avoid those who might feel intimidated or jealous or the nay-sayers who want to be validated for their negativity. You'll also run across people you never dreamed could be of help to you – either with a relationship or resource of theirs.

Keep that vision of what you want to achieve with you always. It will be what keeps the decisions you make on track. And remember to stay flexible – you might want to achieve your goal by going down a certain path — remember that there are lots of ways to get there and just be open to taking roads you never saw coming.

JEAN GALE'S MAKE AHEAD EGGS

Carol Kelly is a former business associate from the New York area whom I've known for over twenty years.. But she's more than that—she has been a caring and loyal friend.

Carol Kelly

We are the kind of friends that see each other only at conferences once or twice a year, but the bond is renewed every time we meet. She writes:

"The following recipe is associated with my early years in management at my former company. My broker and his wife (Jean and Kent Gale) were the sweetest, kindest and most generous people in the world, and still are! Several times a year, they would invite the management team to their lovely, warm home for an early morning meeting. We would all arrive to the aromas of fresh coffee and this delicious baked egg dish in the oven. Their gracious hospitality set the stage for me as to how to behave with people that work for you. It is a lesson that I have never forgotten. Nearly thirty years later, my team tells me how much they love their cozy holiday dinner celebrations at my home."

MAKE
AHEAD
EGGS

INGREDIENTS

2 cups bread cubes

1/2 lb. sharp cheddar cheese, cubed

1/2 stick melted butter

1 cup cubed ham

2 cups milk

3-4 eggs

1 teaspoon dry mustard

PREPARATION

Place half the bread cubes in the bottom of a 9 x 13 baking dish. Top with half of the melted butter, then half of the ham, and finally half of the cheese. Repeat the layers. In a separate bowl, beat eggs, add milk and mustard. Pour over the layers, and refrigerate overnight. The next morning put the baking dish in a container filled with water about half way up the side of the baking dish. Bake at 300 degrees for 1 1/2 hours.

Serves 8

JEFF'S GRILLED BRATWURSTS

Despite numerous requests to my eldest son Jeff to contribute to this book, I have had to search my personal cook books to locate the notes I took as he dictated his method for grilling bratwursts.

Cathy Horvath

He claims he never writes things down as he's cooking, so he is hard pressed to make a contribution. On the one hand, his excuse is plausible because many a good cook prepares meals by taste and not by formula. On the other hand, I'm not sure it's not just a copout. At any rate, I served these brats last week and they were delicious. So much so that I have decided to share the "recipe" with you. So, on behalf of my son, enjoy!

JEFF'S
GRILLED
BRATWURSTS

INGREDIENTS AND PREPARATION

Marinate bratwursts overnight in beer. Put links and beer in a saucepan and boil for no more than 10 minutes. As an option you can add garlic, oregano, and basil to the saucepan as the brats are cooking. Or you can simply use Italian Seasonings. (1 tablespoon per 1 lb. brats.) Remove links and grill.

JOAN'S APRICOT & WHITE CHOCOLATE BISCOTTI

INGREDIENTS

2 3/4 cups sifted flour

1 1/2 cups sugar

1/2 cup butter (cut in pieces)

2 1/2 teaspoons baking powder

1 teaspoon salt

1 teaspoon ginger

6 oz. bag (or half of a 12 oz. bag) white chocolate chips

1 2/3 cups chopped almonds (lightly toasted at 350 degrees for 10 minutes)

2 large eggs

1/4 cup and 1 tablespoon apricot brandy

2 teaspoons almond extract

6 oz. chopped dried apricots

PREPARATION:

Grease and flour a large cookie sheet. Combine first 6 ingredients in food processor. Process to a consistency of fine meal. Add white chocolate and process a bit more. (Leave small bits; do not pulverize chocolate.) Set aside.

In a large bowl, beat eggs with brandy and extracts. Add flour mixture, apricots and nuts. Mix well. Shape into two 18″ logs on cookie sheet. (Log should be about 1 1/2 inches in diameter.) Cover with plastic and refrigerate until firm—about two hours.

Bake at 350 degrees for 20-25 minutes until lightly golden. Remove from oven. Turn oven down to 325 degrees. Cool logs about 15 minutes. Slice to desired thickness. Turn slices on sides. Return to cookie sheet and bake about 10 more minutes.

Yield: about 3 dozen

JOHNNY, THE FAMILY ANGEL

Kathy Masters-Jaeckel

It was a beautiful September day in Chicago. Looking out our apartment window at the vibrant fall colors was a welcomed diversion from the side effects of my pregnancy. Like most pregnant women, I was having a tough time keeping food down. I kept saying to myself that it was worth it, because I was carrying a very active baby boy. Of course back in the '60s, we relied only on mother's intuition to let everyone know what color outfits to buy the anticipated newborn. I was intuitive since I was a young girl. I would talk to Johnny all the time and say, "I know you are a boy and I'm anxious to see you."

I think I was into my sixth or seventh month, when I started dreaming about attending a funeral. I knew it was either John, my husband, or Johnny. I couldn't determine which one it was. I tried to think happy thoughts as I was going to sleep but quite often I would wake up sobbing.

September 11th was a bright sunny day, and it was particularly special because I delivered a beautiful baby boy. I could finally say, "See I told you. It's a BOY!" A few busy months later, my nightmares resumed but now, it was a vision of little Johnny pulling himself up for the first time in his crib. He had a smile on his face as the one side of the crib slipped and he went plummeting to the floor, head first. I would wake up screaming, "Catch him; he's falling!"

Six months later when I put our little sandy haired boy down for a nap in his crib, I pulled up the side and checked it as I always did and began walking out of the room. I had gone about five steps when I heard the squeek of the rail. I turned just in time to see Johnny lean over the top and fall head first. I reached out as I raced across the room towards the crib. My fingertips just grazed the top of his head as he landed partially on my fingertips and mostly on the thick rug under the crib. He whimpered a little and he had a slight bump on his head. I held him in my arms for a long time that afternoon. The dreams of this exact scene stopped immediately but that gut feeling that there was more to come continued. Was it about my husband or my child?

When Johnny was almost two years old, I gave birth to a beautiful baby girl that we named Lynette. She went home in pink and lace that I had purchased weeks before the delivery. (I knew she would be a girl.) Now I wrestled with juggling my time with the children and leaving time for John. For a long time, our marriage wasn't going well, and our relationship continued to deteriorate. When John left for National Guard Training the children and I moved into my parent's home. Eventually we talked things over and John drove us all back into the apartment.

Johnny often felt hot and coughed more frequently than I thought was normal. I discussed this with his doctor and the amount of drugs being prescribed to cure Johnny: "would they destroy his immune system?" The doctor replied, "That could be. Next time I will give him something different, not a prescription medicine."

One day, Johnny's fever hit 104. I called the doctor's office, but it was his day off and he wasn't there. The doctor returned my call and told me to try a tub of lukewarm water with alcohol in it and use aspirin suppositories for the fever. I followed his instructions. Within a couple of hours my little slugger was limp in my arms. I fed him ice chips but there was no response. I called the hospital and asked them to call our doctor. No call back. We drove to the Emergency Room. On the way, little Johnny began to make the most God awful screech. This sound stopped as we arrived at St. Annes Hospital. The same place Johnny and I were born.

The Emergency Room staff said he was probably having a reaction to the aspirin suppository and the fever and I should take him home. I pleaded with them to get my doctor. When they finally did, the doctor said he would meet us back at the hospital at 6:30 AM. That was several hours from then. I asked other doctors to look at him. "I know there is something really wrong with my child. He is not responding to me." They couldn't touch him because he was another doctor's patient. We returned home.

I stayed up with him the rest of the night. When we returned to the hospital at the appointed hour, our doctor was not in sight. Frightened and frustrated, I called my parents and sister. My sister suggested a consultation of doctors. My doctor finally arrived. I demanded consultation with other doctors, and testing. My parents summoned their neighbor who worked at the hospital. He was a tech for EEGs which is a brain wave test. By this time the doctors were saying he was dying and were not sure why. After the test, the neighbor said there is still some activity. He may pull through. My mom suggested we go home and take a shower and get a little rest. She and my dad offered to stay in the waiting room. By now Johnny was in the Intensive Care Unit. We weren't allowed much time to see him. I was afraid to leave but I was totally exhausted and kept falling off the bedside chair as I dozed off. Mom said he will probably pull through this. I said, "No Mom. I am so afraid that this is what I have known for most of his life. I think he is going to die." We cried and held onto each other.

We took the short drive home but it seemed like forever. I shook with exhaustion and struggled to walk up the stairs to our apartment. We opened the door. The phone rang. We looked at each other. John motioned to me to pick up the phone. I did. It was Mom. "Johnny just died, honey. Come back to the hospital." I cannot describe what it was like to walk into a hospital room where your child who is almost four years old is laying on a cold metal cart, uncovered and lifeless. The autopsy said it was either Ryes Syndrome or Encephalitis. They didn't know. Later I read that aspirin with a high fever can cause the symptoms he had. The brain had swollen to 25% of its normal size.

One year after Johnny's death I delivered a healthy baby boy we named Kevin John. He grew up, married and has 2 sons, born 36 and 38 years after Johnny died. I knew Kevin would be a boy and I knew he would have 2 sons of his own. Heather was born almost three years after Kevin. She was and still is a blonde haired, blue eyed beauty. She now has two beautiful children; a boy and a girl. And, I guessed right on what they would be also.

The experience of my child's death changed my life. I came to realize the other side of existence is so close. We just have to allow ourselves to experience a higher form of ourselves. We all have a Higher Self. It is that which is connected to our lighter form and our soul. I found when I meditated deeply, I could lift myself into a place of higher consciousness and understand life and death from a whole new perspective.

It took many years of psychology courses, metaphysical classes, and prayers to get to the point where I was ready to learn how to reach Johnny on the other side. This had been my goal since he died. John had no interest in this kind of information and help. There is no need to give the details here so I will just say, John and I were divorced when our youngest, Heather, was almost three. I am so glad I had no idea how hard it would be, to be a single mom with three children. But once I was committed to it, I went forward and only looked back a few brief times.

The adjustment period of losing a son and divorcing a husband depends on how quickly you release your anger. I mean the deep down, gut-wrenching anger. Once you have begun the process of releasing it, you can go on to the next step which is understanding why such a small perfect child of God should have to leave you. During my angry stage, I hated God. I asked, "How could you do this to me?"

After the divorce, I found time to study about God, the Universe, Life after death, Meditation, Channeling, Past lifetimes, Past life regression, Rebirthing and most of all, why do some people leave this planet and go back home to God so early in life. After a couple years of joining groups that taught how to let go of pain and how to meditate and pray deeply, I emerged as a Metaphysical leader and intuitive counselor who could help others move through their emotional and physical blocks.

I still shed some tears on the anniversary of Johnny's birthday. However, that deep aching heart pain is no longer there and I go about working with others in their various journeys of drawing closer to God and to the other side. I am now extremely happy. My husband, Larry, and I designed and built a Bed and Breakfast in Sedona, Arizona. It's called Sedona Cathedral Hideaway Bed & Breakfast. We welcome people in their journeys. We grow in our love. My three children are adults with their own families. Life is good."

JUDGE NOT

This is a tough one for me to share, but it has been the most powerful lesson in my life.

Cathy Horvath

My dear friend Connie Siewert and I founded an organization called The Eclectic Ladies Network. We invited women we met from all over the Atlanta Metro area. We sought out women who were so unique and so interesting in their experiences, personalities and/or professions that we would want to take them to lunch and just listen to them share something about themselves. Instead of a one-on-one lunch, we hold a monthly pot luck luncheon which is highlighted by a thought provoking question that is answered in a round-robin fashion. On this particular day, after a fabulous lunch enjoyed by about 25 women of all ages, backgrounds, religions and race, the question was posed, "Who was your mentor and what did you learn?"

I was stumped by that one because I never had a mentor. I always wished I had someone to turn to other than my parents, but that was not the case for me. I was getting nervous as each person shared some wonderful stories of their fifth grade teacher, a neighbor, a corporate executive, a college professor, etc. I started to feel a little intimidated by the responses but the more I thought about my life, I suddenly realized that my son, Chris, was my mentor. He still is to this day. In living through our challenges with his mental illness, I learned never to judge a street person, someone who seems "odd" or anyone else for that matter. Here is my story about Chris:

The third of four children in our family, Chris was a bright spot in my life. When he was born, his older brother was 6 and his big sister was 8 and both attended grammar school. Realizing how quickly they had grown, I was determined to cherish each moment with this little one. He and I had a good time together. He was a beautiful little boy who never gave me an ounce of trouble. He even slept through the night after he was born! (I would get up several times anyway to check his breathing.) However, as he progressed through grammar school, his deportment became a real issue. He was smart, but he was a bit rowdy. His teachers and principal kept telling my husband and me that he was an intelligent student but he was a distraction in the classroom. Grounding him and taking away his favorite toys didn't seem to faze him. We kept hoping he would grow out of this stage. He wasn't much of a student in high school either, but the responses from his teachers were that he's a good kid and will grow out of this phase of his life like all teens do. When things didn't change much, we began family counseling sessions with him. Three psychologists and thousands of dollars later, we saw no improvement. But we kept up with the sessions, during which we did all the talking and he just sat in his chair motionless.

Then a strange thing happened. In his senior year, his hair turned into tight curls as though he had a permanent. He and my husband would get into arguments because my husband accused him of perming his hair. Chris would deny it saying over and over again, "Dad, I'm telling you the truth!" Then we noticed his hands would tremble so badly that he couldn't pick up peas from his dinner plate with a fork. Something was definitely wrong. I took him to our family doctor. He tested him and suggested he quit drinking so much cola and smoking fewer cigarettes. Chris graduated high school and tried junior college. When that didn't work out, he landed a few jobs but couldn't hold on to them. We didn't think much of it because we figured at some point he would find his niche and everything would work out. WRONG!! Note: what we learned later on was that the change in Chris' hair, which remains curly to this day at age 41, reflected the chemical change that was going on inside his body.

The week after his 21st birthday, we drove him to a well known mental hospital in the western suburbs of Chicago. He sat up front and I sat in the back of the car watching him as Ray and I convinced him that he needed help. You see, for most of the past week while on a family vacation, he was in a catatonic state. My son-in-law and the other children knew something was wrong. Chris was lost somewhere deep inside of himself. He agreed to seek help. He had to because now he was 21 and legally in charge of his life. Chris voluntarily entered the mental institution. The family sessions were awful. First words out of the psychiatrists' mouths were questions directed to me. Was he a planned pregnancy? Did I try to abort? Did I take drugs or drink large quantities of alcohol during my pregnancy? Although I was ready to throw a few punches, I truthfully stated that we tried for two years to conceive him and no, I led a very healthy lifestyle minus drugs or any kind or alcohol. We visited Chris as often as family was allowed and so did his brother. Not surprising, the counselors there would tell us what a perfect and helpful patient he was. He was well liked by all, but his condition was barely stabilized. He was hospitalized for three weeks and sent home with a variety of drugs. He was diagnosed as Schizophrenic with a severe psychotic disorder. I will tell you, that was a blow to my heart! I didn't even know what those words meant. I never heard them before. The head of the hospital told me he would never be normal and would be this way for the rest of his life. I went through Hell when Chris would call me at my office begging me to help him get released. His voice would crack from trying to hold back tears. If he cried perhaps I would think he really did need help, you see. We would talk, and I would plead with him to give it just another week. I promised—just another week. So he stuck it out. As tough as these years were for the family, it was not an easy time for Chris either. Shortly after a three week stay, he was released and we took him home.

A few years later, through an organization called NAMI (National Alliance on Mental Illness) my husband and I took an eight week course. It was offered to family members of the "clients" to help them better understand the nature of mental illness, the possible causes, and most importantly to learn what our son was going through. He couldn't help but ask "Out of the four kids, why me, Mom?" Taking that course was the best thing we ever did. We learned that Chris was right on target time-wise. Mental illness strikes kids in post adolescence and early twenties. Straight A students are suddenly severely depressed and/or attempt suicide. These people are not weirdoes; they suffer from a chemical imbalance. Mental illness is a disease just like Diabetes, Parkinson's, Multiple Sclerosis, etc. That was 20 years ago, and not much was being done to understand this terrible disease. Things are a lot different now. New research offers new approaches along with new drugs to help. But as yet, there is no cure. "Clients" are stabilized as best as possible but not cured. I highly recommend NAMI to anyone who struggles to better understand mental illness.

All together, Chris has had six hospitalizations. The last one was in 2010. Several years ago, he completed a two year Electronic Technician course at DeVry University. (A fete the head of the mental hospital swore he could never accomplish.) He held down two electronic jobs after that and seemed to be doing okay. But during the months following our move to Atlanta with my job transfer, his condition deteriorated. He called us several times a day and we encouraged him in his efforts to lead a "normal" life. He tried so hard. We'd send him money to bail him out of a financial bind as often as we could. He didn't handle his money very well and would often get himself into such debt he finally had to declare bankruptcy. (That's all part of the illness, we discovered.)

Through the efforts of the psychiatrist he was seeing, he received Social Security Disability Income because he really wasn't capable of holding a job sufficient to support himself. Long story short, and it is a very long story, he wound up in shelters run by churches and other nonprofit organizations. Sometimes, when the SS check ran out, he slept in vacant buildings or wherever he could find shelter. But he would still keep the lines of communication open. My son Jeff and his wife Kim invited Chris to dinner from time to time and sent him home with bags of groceries. Chris called us three and even four times a day. I worried about him but he always told me not to worry, that he is holding his own.

And now for the miracle. God works in mysterious ways and with a purpose. I am unwavering in that belief. Here's why: Two years into the job for which I was transferred to Atlanta, I was laid off. By a strange sequence of events (oh, really?), I was hired by a company that asked me to live in OakBrook, IL, a Western suburb of Chicago. I was asked to stay for about three months to help stabilize an acquisition that was not going well. Having lived in that area all my life and knowing the industry they were involved in, I was a perfect candidate for the job. So I took the assignment and commuted there from Atlanta. I was put up in a lovely corporate apartment while I concentrated on the job at hand. Then the miracle fell into place. The calls from Chris began to slow down until we didn't hear from him for over three weeks. My mother's intuition kicked in and I just knew something was wrong. I asked my husband to drive up for the weekend to help locate him. He was supposedly living on the streets or in shelters in a deteriorating town about 35 miles to the south of where I worked and lived.

We spent all day Saturday speaking to people at the shelters where he stayed from time to time. They would direct us to the library where many street people hung out, or to hotels for the indigent but we couldn't find him. I now know what parents go through when their child has been abducted. We knew he was out there somewhere but we just couldn't find him. We drove up one street and down another. We asked people if they saw him. Many people knew him and would give us hints. But no Chris – until the counselor at the Salvation Army shelter suggested we come back for the 5 o'clock supper that was offered to the homeless. Chris often showed up there for a meal. So we returned about 45 minutes before 5 P.M. and sat in the car I had rented for my job and watched as carloads of families showed up and waited in the hot sun to be fed. Women in wheelchairs, mothers with toddlers, and lots of weather-worn street people. It was in the high 90's that day. A car drove up behind us and remained parked there until the doors to the shelter opened. I looked in the rear view mirror as the car approached the back of ours and I commented to Ray how the man in the passenger seat reminded me of Chris as he slept so soundly with his head tilted back and his mouth wide open. Well, the older woman who was the driver finally got out and entered the building. The man stayed behind still sleeping. I finally asked Ray to go inside to check to see if we had missed Chris or if anyone there knew where we might find him. Just as Ray left my sight, the man from the car got out and headed for the door. I watched him, but I didn't recognize him until I saw him from the back and recognized his walk. It was Chris! It was our Chris! I beeped the horn but he didn't hear me. I couldn't get out of the car fast enough to catch up with him before he entered the building. When I finally entered the hallway to the dining room, Ray was coming out of the door and Chris was sandwiched in between us. Needless to say, he was shocked to see us. He wouldn't let me hug him because he was filthy with grease and grime from days living on the streets without a shower. So I said to him, "Want to come home Chris?" And he did, without hesitation.

Now here's the important part I ask you to remember in this whole story: Chris was a street person so filthy and grimy that I didn't recognize him. Yet when we took him back to my apartment and he showered and shaved and dressed in Ray's Nautica shirt and Tommy Hilfiger jeans, he looked every bit like a handsome young man, probably into computer programming or software sales. You would never know. Street people are not all druggies or alcoholics or bums. Some are just down on their luck, and some are struggling with mental illness without a family or friend to help them out. You just don't know.

There is so much more to this story it would fill a book, but the best part is that Chris lives in an apartment in the Atlanta area and is associated with a non-profit organization that is called The Vistas Group, a program supported by Northside Hospital. Chris has had many guardian angels help him since moving here with us. This organization is full of them. Until his last hospitalization in the fall of 2010, he worked part time as Facility Assistant at the Buckhead AMC Theatre. He fixed their electronic equipment, painted walls and floors, and repaired just about everything and anything. He is articulate, intelligent, and quite artistic. He sketches beautiful and unique designs for us to keep. What is so special about Chris is that he has a very kind heart. He is generous and thoughtful. He's never been angry towards his dad or me, and is always eager to come to the house to help his dad with projects. In short, he is a very good soul. I think he has come to earth to teach me and our family about judging others, and to stand up for the cause of mental illness. I'm glad he's ours.

Chris has read this story and has given me permission to share it with you. I wouldn't do it otherwise.

KATHY'S POWER WINTER SMOOTHIE

Sedona Cathedral Hideaway
www.SedonaCathedralHideaway.com
1-866-9Sedona

Kathy Masters-Jaeckel

KATHY'S POWER
WINTER
SMOOTHIE

INGREDIENTS AND PREPARATION

Use a blender with a blade for frozen food.

1. Add 1 1/2 cups cold, purified water to a blender

2. Pour in 3/4 capfuls Liquid Vitamins-Minerals

3. Open up one Ester C Capsule. Pour into liquid

4. Add one heaping tablespoon Flaxseed Meal

5. Add 1/2 teaspoon Very Green

6. Add a nectarine, peach or 1/4 of a mango

7. Add approximately 1 1/2 cups frozen fruit of your choice
   (passion fruit has higher sugar, carbs and calories)
   Option: add a splash of orange juice

8. Liquefy on high for about 1 or 2 minutes (quality of your
   blender determines the time) until all pieces are liquefied

9. Add 3/4 capful of a protein powder. Liquefy until frothy.

KNOW YOUR PLACE

Cathy Horvath

I grew up in a blue collar family and lived in a blue collar neighborhood. My parents raised us with strong morals and ethics. Mother cautioned us to "know our place." She seemed to be intimidated by those who were wealthy or more educated than she. I married and eventually moved out to the Western suburbs of Chicago. My friends and I made a special day of shopping at an upscale mall called Oakbrook, located in a wealthy suburb west of the city. We would don our best garb including heels and white gloves. Do you believe it, to go to a mall!? That was many, many years ago. Back to the story. Even though I dressed to the nines, and looked every bit the part of a well-to-do shopper, I couldn't bring myself to walk through the doors of a high-end department store called Bonwit Teller. (It has long since gone out of business.) I felt I had "to know my place" and didn't feel I had the right to look around because I could never afford even the least expensive item on the shelves. I thought the clerks would know that and would watch me as I strolled through the departments, and I would be very embarrassed if I didn't buy something.

A couple of years passed. I visited the mall quite often, but never the Bonwit Teller store. Then I relayed my experience to a friend of mine, and he admonished me for being so intimidated. "You aren't going to be arrested for browsing through the store," he said. "Next time you're there, march right through those doors and have a look around. You have every right to browse as anyone else." Well, I was still hesitant to take his advice until one Sunday our Pastor made an interesting comment during his sermon. The subject was Prosperity. Among his many suggestions for attracting prosperity into one's life was to watch what wealthy, successful people do. Go to where they shop; absorb the energy of prosperity in the upscale shops. Go to BONWIT TELLER and Nieman Marcus. Look around, feel the energy of wealth," he said. He specifically mentioned Bonwit Teller! It was as though the Universe was trying to tell me something.

Later that year I saw an ad that the store ran for a part time position as a clerk during the Christmas season. It really took a lot of courage to think they would consider hiring me, but I took a deep breath and approached the Personnel Dept. I was hired immediately and enjoyed two successful holiday seasons in the gift dept. It was great fun and I assisted many wealthy customers with their selections. It was such a nice experience that a few years later I was not hesitant at all in applying for the position of Bridal Manager.

KNOW YOUR PLACE

Since I had recently spent a couple years as a bridal consultant, I was hired. It was a wonderful job helping brides find their special gown, and I especially enjoyed buying trips to New York and Chicago. I even managed to purchase a few things in the store every now and then. The employee discount helped a lot with that. Most importantly I began to realize I would never allow myself to be intimidated like that again. No one, nothing can make me feel unworthy. That was a huge lesson, but one I have long remembered as I ventured through the corporate world. Learning that lesson early on was a big help.

Sometimes it is difficult for many people to believe in something that they cannot see, feel or taste. These folks close their minds to the possibility of a loving entity being with them all the time. They don't recognize happenings – little and big – in their daily lives that can be attributed to Angels.

Alison Kelly

Many of us have images of Angels sitting on clouds, playing harps and smiling down on children. Actually, Angels have jobs. Angels have specific missions and work hard to guide us toward the "Light" of which we are all a part. The energy of Angels surrounds us at all times. They never desert us. They are there for us always. They desire nothing more than to guide us toward what is good and protect us from that which will cause harm. Because as humans, we have free will, Angels are restricted by what they can do; which is nothing if we do not ask them. The only time an Angel may help without being specifically asked is if we're in danger and it's not our time to go. It is neither wrong nor selfish to ask for your Angel's help, as the Bible states: "For He shall give His Angels charge over you, to keep you in all the ways. (Psalm 91:11)" We were given the gift of Angels and they want us to use that gift!

I have been talking to God and my Angels for many years and have helped many people learn how to talk to their Angels, too. Angels can help with your health, life purpose, relationships, business and illnesses. Open up to the Angelic energy in your life. There is a whole divine support system at work behind the scenes right now.

I am sharing this information with the readers of this book as well as those who visit my web site: www.KnowingAngels.com. I am telling you what I know from my own personal experience. This is my story.

Life was good. I was a healthy young mother of three in 2000. I taught fitness classes; my husband had a job and I lived a spirit filled life. What more could one want? Well, that was all about to change.

It all began with a slight tingling in my toes. I thought my shoes were too tight, so I loosened them. Then the tingle turned into numbness, but I ignored it. The numbness spread from the toes to the shins and around to my calves. "What in the world," I wondered. Surely I had a pinched nerve in my back. A trip to the chiropractor should solve everything I thought. Then, okay, maybe two trips, or maybe three. Then my thighs were numb and I was beginning to get irritated. I decided to go to a back specialist. His assessment confirmed my own diagnosis as a pinched nerve.

An MRI was done on my lower back and lumbar spine. Everything looked fine, but it wasn't really. The numbness began to encompass my entire lower body. Even a flame held to my flesh caused a vicious wound but not one grimace of pain. The doctor administered three rounds of anti-inflammatory shots directly into the epidural space of my spinal cord. Not fun—no help! Even a shower was a surreal experience. I saw the water hitting my legs but I could not feel the water. It had been about two months since the first slight tingle in my toes. Since then the tingle had taken over half of my body. Everything from my chest down was numb and cold. I was rapidly losing muscle control. Every step I took required my full concentration. Holding my bladder was also beginning to be a challenge. I then began a two week long spiral downward into depression and desperation. Although the doctors were convinced that my problem stemmed from my lower back and probably was caused by stress, I could clearly feel a block of energy in my upper back.

I spent what some would call "The Dark Night of the Soul" during which I meditated, prayed and asked for guidance. After many hours of prayers and tears, I finally received a message from my Angels telling me that I needed an upper back MRI. The next morning I phoned my doctor's office for an appointment and insisted he order a full spinal MRI. With insurance approval, of course, I had the test. Almost as soon as I left the facility, I received a call from the radiologist. "You have the biggest spinal cord tumor we've ever seen. Get to a doctor immediately," he said. I opened the phone book to find a neurosurgeon and was guided to a name unfamiliar to me. The miracles began to happen:

I phoned the neurosurgeon's office and fully expected a long wait for an appointment. However, the office had just had a cancellation. I could see the doctor immediately. And then came the moment of change of who I was forever. After examining me, viewing my MRI, and asking me questions, my neurosurgeon explained that the paralysis already caused by this tumor was most likely permanent and the tumor needed to come out as soon as possible. He continued: my spinal cord was probably permanently damaged and I would not regain what bodily functions I had already lost. He also warned me that the surgery was very risky. There was the possibility of my spinal cord being completely severed upon the removal of the tumor. It was likely that I would require the use of a wheelchair for the rest of my life. Furthermore, if the tumor was malignant I had about eighteen months to live. Alas, his schedule was full and he could not perform the surgery for two more weeks. For two weeks I sat in my house, hardly able to walk, and not able to feel my legs. I wondered if I would ever get to see my children grow.

It was time to go to work on myself. It seemed that everything I had ever learned about energy healing was all for this moment. I began to live in a state of humble gratitude and appreciation.

I spent time in prayer, meditation, and silence. I channeled healing energy from Divine Source and removed the source that was causing my tumor to grow. Heavenly Angels never left my side and showed me how to repair my spinal cord. During those two weeks leading up to the scheduled surgery, I experienced a place of peace and serenity that I had only dreamed about. I "Let Go and Let God." I meditated on the tumor and visualized the spinal cord coming back whole and healthy. I forgave the tumor and thanked it for giving me two weeks with God. I felt no fear and no hate. I didn't feel that I was under attack from the tumor. I sent it unconditional love. I surrendered the outcome and stayed in a state of peace.

Well, nothing short of a miracle occurred on that potentially fateful day of my operation. As I was being prepped for surgery and hooked up to a computer, the nurses asked me if I were a celebrity because there were so many people in the operating room. The fact was that I was so young and the tumor was so big was something for the medical personnel to behold. Several hours later I woke up in the recovery room and was able to wiggle my toes and to feel my body again. The nurses had tears in their eyes and were saying "We didn't think you would make it. You should have seen that surgery.

The surgeon removed your vertebrae, exposed your spinal cord, and cut it open 6 inches. Then he spent 5 hours "unwrapping" that tumor from inside your cord. Amazing!" Yes, it was amazing, and the tumor was not malignant. I was going to live!

There were two miracles that took place for me. One was getting my physical body back but the second was even greater and much more unexpected. I was going to live! Suddenly, everything and everyone around me looked brighter. I could see life clearer. Things that once seemed important were now trivial in comparison to the greatest gift of all—life. The devastation of developing a life threatening illness ultimately transformed into something quite remarkable—a new perspective and even greater appreciation for myself and love for God. There is a shift in spirit on the deepest soul level when you are faced with the reality of your own mortality. This powerful experience also allowed me to trust what I have known for years: that God and the Angels have unconditional love for every living thing and their love can be used for profound healing. They taught me how to prepare myself for healing when combined with the efforts of the medical practitioners. They have inspired me to help others.

Light blessings….Alison

LAUREN'S LOLLIPOP SUGAR COOKIES

Lauren Huber

Lauren is my eighteen year old granddaughter. Not to be out done by her sister Ashley's contribution to this book, she has asked her Mom to explain how her favorite birthday cookie is made.

For Lauren's classmates' "treats" on her birthday, she requested sugar cookie lollipops almost every year. It's quite easy: prior to baking a big sugar cookie, insert a popsicle stick. After cooling, each lollipop cookie can be decorated with the birthday year of celebration. At times, my daughter Robyn even added colorful ribbons to the sticks. Lauren loved decorating them, and her classmates looked forward to her birthday treat.

LEARNING TO TELL THE TRUTH

I was a nun for 20 years in an Upstate New York Franciscan community, but my sense of honesty came about long before I entered their community

Dr. Mary Hilaire Tavenner

at the age of 17. My mother and father taught me to be fair, kind, compassionate and honest… and if at all possible, keep a sense of humor while doing it.

I think many of us can look into our past and discover some of those "defining moments" when we chose to become a better person; when we morphed into a better character; when we learned to make better choices.

Recently I completed a biography of my mother's life, entitled *Memories of Mom: They called her "Dutch"*. In that book I share many of the family stories, but did not include the following. There is no greater an influence in our lives than our parents, no more powerful an example. Parents should, above everything else, understand that parenting is the most important job we have in life, and it should not be embarked upon lightly, nor by the faint of heart.

I am one of 7 children. When I was about 9, my brother and I were having lunch at home and usually we would both walk back to school after we ate. This particular day my brother wanted to return early and my mother drove him back to school. I was home alone. I found a candle in the kitchen drawer and decided to light it. Then I went to use the bathroom upstairs, and decided it was getting late and that I had better leave for school, forgetting the candle aglow in the kitchen.

After school, my father declared, "I came home from work to find a candle burning in the kitchen! Who left it there?" I was too afraid to tell on myself, so he lined us all up in the living room, and all had proof of their innocence, except me. Several had been in high school, several were at work, and Patrick had left for school early when my mom offered him a ride back to school.

There it was! I was caught in a lie. It was obvious to Dad and to all, I was the culprit. I was never punished for my untruth, but had to sit at the supper table with my siblings and parents, all of them knowing I was a liar. It was awful. I was so ashamed, and never wanted to lie again.

But I did… in high school, when my Spanish teacher asked all in the class to raise their hands if they did not have their homework finished. I didn't want to tell on myself. (I guess you might call it "Pleading the Fifth".) A few (obviously, more honest) souls raised their hands and admitted to not having completed their homework for class. Then my Spanish teacher went around the class to check our work, and when he came to me he asked, "Where is your homework?" I had to admit I did not have it. So, he said out loud to the entire class, "You're obviously a liar! Anyone who lies is a cheat and a thief as well." That really embarrassed me. Still, I felt he was probably right. I could tell the other kids felt sorry for me. They were not so harsh in their judgment. So, I learned early in life not to lie. I obviously needed the refresher course in high school.

After graduation, I entered the convent with a desire to never lie again. After twenty years with the nuns I decided to leave. You might say that I "kicked the habit." I've never regretted that decision. I'm in my 60's now, and as I look back on my life I have to say I never want to lie to anyone, ever, about anything. Whoever came up with the quip, "Honesty is the best policy" certainly knew what s/he was talking about!

That isn't to say I tell people they are stupid when they are stupid, or tell people they are fat when they are fat. I just don't bring up unkind thoughts. Most people know their shortcomings, and they who haven't figured them out, probably will, given a lifetime.

For some of my favorite convent yarns, read my books: *Nun of This and Nun of That: Books One and Two*. You might think I'm fabricating stories about "the good ol' days," but I'm not. Life is stranger than fiction. That's another one of my favorite truisms.

Dr. Mary Hilaire Tavenner
www.dutchink.com
dutchink@aol.com
(440) 288-0416

LESSONS FROM MY MOM

Cathy Horvath

"If you do not have the opportunity to do great things, you can do small things in a great way." When I first read that quotation a few years ago, I thought of my mom immediately. It seemed to explain how she lived her life. Not one to demand the spotlight, she held that spotlight nevertheless in the hearts of those whose lives she touched.

We come to this earthly existence with a unique set of attributes, strengths and weaknesses. Yet we can't help being influenced by our childhood experiences and the roles our parents played. I see a bit of Mom in each of her three daughters.

Christmas is a big thing around our homes. Just like Mom, my sisters and I spend days fussing over our respective family trees and all the decorations to welcome our visitors. I remember our big trees, real ones, that Mom would have Dad plug with extra branches to give it a perfect shape. Dad and Mom put on the lights. We kids would help with the ornaments, small ones at the top and then graduating in size until the larger ones hung at the bottom. But Mom and only Mom would put the tinsel on, one strand at a time until the tree literally dripped in silver. That's Mom—creating a warm and inviting home that said "welcome, make yourself at home" to our visitors.

Patience for details to make it right. "If you're going to do something, do it right or don't do it at all" she would say. How many times have I repeated that to my four children!

We're creative—each of us. One sister can go in her yard, gather a collection of various sprigs, berries and greenery and create the loveliest of centerpieces. Mom loved to wander through the vacant lots adjacent to her house and pick beautiful ferns and flowers to fill a basket. That same sister is a great cook, too. Mom could always be found in the kitchen—that was her domain. I'm a kitchen diva. Even though I'm in my "Sunset years" I still get excited over a new cook book, take cooking classes, and am a devotee of the Food Network.

We're each a caring and supportive friend—my other sister is always there for family members in crisis just like Mom was. When our cousin Joe passed away from cancer in Arizona, she stepped in and helped with the arrangements, including his remarriage to his estranged wife a few weeks before passing. She has been an incredible help to our elder family members and others who have needed her take charge attitude and her willingness to put their needs before hers. That is just like our mom in action.

She was a loving mother. I was 10 years old when my youngest sister was born. From that day on I was Mom's right hand girl. Making formula, changing diapers, washing bottles, sleepless nights— those times taught me that motherhood isn't about dressing up live dolls. It's a serious undertaking and a lot of hard work. The role is not without heartaches, worry, pride, and love—lots of love. For twenty five years I have tried to emulate her love and devotion to her grandchildren. Her world revolved around them and they adored her.

One thing I learned from my mother: It isn't the riches we've accumulated or the titles we've earned that mean anything when we leave this life, but the legacy of love we leave behind. I believe God welcomed her home with the greeting "Well done, my daughter, Heaven awaits you."

LESSONS LEARNED FROM THE CORPORATE WORLD

In preparing for this book, I revisited events from childhood all the way through adulthood.

Cathy Horvath

I realized that I came away from many of those experiences learning something about myself, or about life that I carried with me as I moved into each new year. Here is an example of a memory associated with a life lesson while I was a member of the corporate world.

While Vice President of a large real estate division in the Chicago area, I frequently interacted with another executive in the corporate offices. I was totally unprepared for the chauvinistic, egotistical, and condescending man, especially on a professional basis. Get the picture? My stomach would churn every time I had to interact with him. Angry and frustrated, I sought out a friend who had been my spiritual counselor. We talked for a long time and I got it all out of my system. I

have to admit, I really didn't expect this solution from her. Her suggestion: "Bless him." "Bless him?!" "Yes, that's right. Bless him every time you see him for showing you firsthand how never, ever to act. How not to treat another human being. Without him to remind you, you might one day slip into that same mode. Now you won't." From then on, whenever he was around, I mentally blessed him. The words kind of stuck at first, but I got the hang of it. I even managed to giggle inside my head whenever our paths crossed. He didn't have a clue what a wonderful life lesson he was providing! I've used that lesson many times over and not just with him. I now realize that many people who cross our paths in life have come to provide us with a lesson. Some lessons are obvious—others take a little more work to figure out—like this one.

LESSONS LEARNED IN CABO SAN LUCAS

Deborah Hill (www.AwarenessInitiative.com) has been actively involved in the coaching,

Deborah Hill

counseling and training of others throughout her adult life. She began her career as a Registered Nurse and Nurse-Midwife. However, her life's journey evolved into becoming an intuitive coach, counselor, author, speaker, instructor and energetic therapist. Her extensive experiences include four degrees in science and psychology, 30 years of property management and investment, and 20 years as an entrepreneur and president of her own business. Her story is as remarkable as her life experiences.

"It was 1975 and the road from California through Baja California had just opened. The scenery was magnificent. The peninsula is quite unique in that it is surrounded by the Pacific Ocean on the west side and the Sea of Cortez on the east side. My friend Perry and I put all of our supplies into my station wagon and drove south from beach to beach. We swam for hours along the way. We saw very few people as we traveled.

After two weeks of driving and swimming our way south, we ended up on a beach in Cabo San Lucas. At the time, it was a small city barely developed. There was one hotel and miles of glorious beach. At the tip of the peninsula stood a unique and exquisite landmark (a combination of rock formations and islands). The tip is all rocks. Just beyond that rocky point is a small island that is inhabited by seals—lots and lots of seals. It's quite a scene, but oh the noise and smell! High in the air just beyond that site is a huge rock slab in the shape of an arch that connects the mainland with another small island. The rock formation is called El Arco. That area is quite famous and often used in photo shoots.

Perry and I were adventurers and by now great swimmers. We drove to the tip and waded into the warm, blue waters, and swam towards El Arco. We swam past the seals and under the glorious arch. It was an experience I'll never forget.

Just beyond El Arco was a huge boulder that we couldn't swim around. Instead, there was a crevice going through it. We let the tide carry us forward and held the sides to brace ourselves when the current went the other way. We made our way through and were greeted on the other side by a tiny, white sand beach. Lovely. We were tired by then and fell asleep there, listening to the waves and reveling in our experience.

We awoke an hour or so later and immediately sensed that something was different. The tide had changed. The beach was smaller, the water was rougher. We knew we had to get back soon and began swimming. As we neared the entrance to the rock crevice I felt something that I'd never experienced or dreamed of. I was sucked down by the undercurrent. Looking up from about 45 feet below I knew I didn't have enough air to make it to the surface. I wasn't scared or upset. I felt calm as I realized that I was going to die.

I was wrong. A miracle happened. Immediately I felt the water surround me firmly. It felt like two hands cupping me from the front and back like a child would hold a newly caught butterfly. The hands quickly and efficiently propelled me up to the surface and gently delivered me onto the adjoining rock. I followed the motion and climbed up. As I turned I saw Perry on a nearby rock, arms raised to dive in, eyes like saucers, mouth wide open and face white.

There was nothing to say. We both got the lesson. Actually, two of them. #1: Don't mess with nature. #2: There is a higher force and we are taken care of. No doubt!

The impact of the experience left us speechless. But we soon realized we were stuck because we could no longer return through the crevice in the rock. But we weren't stuck for long. Within minutes, a Mexican tour guide came by in a small, motorized row boat. He had one person on board and was yelling at us in Spanish. We couldn't understand what he was saying exactly, but it was obviously something like, 'You stupid Americans. What are you doing there? Get in the boat right now.' So we did. And he took us back to shore.

There's more. We were so very hungry. Out of the rocks on the beach emerged, like a camel in a desert, an American female tourist holding a paper bag. She held the bag out to us saying, "They gave me this sandwich at the hotel and I'm not hungry. Do you want it?" Speechless, we shook our heads yes. The grace and support of the Almighty is never ending, efficient and complete.

That happened 32 years ago. I've lived my life propelled by this experience. In the same way that the hands of the water propelled me up onto the rocks, my spirit was propelled on its journey towards further understanding of this universal force and my connection to it. And, I am further propelled to help others know and understand that no matter what happens I know that I/we are not alone. We are supported and loved."

LIFE'S STEPPING STONES

Cathy Horvath

Several years ago I read a book about personal and spiritual growth that encouraged the reader to create and analyze his/her own personal life timeline to help view one's life more objectively. I jotted down the significant events, turning points, and key influences on my life from my birth to the present. As I listed both negative and positive experiences, I gained insight about myself and my career. I concluded that all my experiences, all the people I'd met along the way, and all the jobs I've had were stepping stones that brought me to where I am today. I realized I did what I had to do each and every day to arrive at my current destination.

First, I was a stay at home Mom. Keeping a clean house, washing clothes on Monday, ironing (yes, we used to do that) on Tuesday, baking on Wednesday, running miscellaneous errands on Thursday, grocery shopping on Fridays, and church on Sundays. I know, I left out Saturday—that was the play day. I took care of my family.

Then, there was the real estate sales woman when I turned 39 and my fourth child was in preschool. My life got a little more complicated then as I juggled career and family. As my career evolved into the corporate relocation industry, my life got even more complicated because then I started to travel for client presentations and conferences. I had to keep connected to the family while preparing to give a speech before hundreds of people the next day, or taking the executives of a multi-national organization out to lunch. It was challenging to receive phone calls from home that told of car accidents, poor report cards, sickness or plumbing problems. I know you get the drift. Many of you have been there, done that or are doing all that now.

My career evolved until I became Vice President of Corporate Services for two of the largest real estate companies in Chicago. We handled the most relocation activity in the country at that time. Now I had a staff to manage and mentor. Now I had a lot more bosses to report to—from clients to the Sr. Vice President to the President to the CEO of my company. But I did it. I kept my family going too.

There's a point to this story. When I finally left my career behind to find my next adventure in life, I looked back to see what I was qualified for in order to take a new direction. What were my skills and experiences that would be a match for something new? I went back to the timeline exercise. What a surprise! What I realized was that all the turning points, personal and career challenges, people, and job responsibilities played a part in shaping the person I am today. I didn't have the time or I didn't take the time then to realize what was happening—I just kept keeping on.

In this journey, I learned that even the not-so-pleasant experiences and the not-so-nice people I encountered were instrumental in formulating my work ethics and personal values. Not only have I learned what to do, but what not to do as well. So much of what happens in one's life has a good purpose, if you can put a positive spin on it and hold to that thinking. I'm now what some would call a "senior citizen" but I'm not done yet! God didn't bring me this far, with all that I've learned and experienced, to dump me now. I've embarked on a new venture with my personal timeline intact, ready for new experiences and probably new lessons too. I am somewhat a stranger to this hi tech world we live in and I wait excitedly to see what each tomorrow will bring.

LINDA LAIRD'S HUMMINGBIRD CAKE

My husband Greg and I met and fell in love at Murray State University in Kentucky in the 1960's. We married in June of our senior year and within eight weeks were living in Rommelshausen, Germany. Greg was a Second Lieutenant in the Army and had arrived a few weeks before I did.

Linda Laird

The first night I arrived I started settling into our small apartment in a German home. There was no phone, no television and I had no car. Greg was stationed thirteen long and windy miles away at Budigen Army Kasern. Within twenty four hours of my arrival, Greg was called away for months to the East/West German border town of Grafenwohr. I never felt so alone in my life and I was really scared. Here I was…in a foreign country, in a strange town, I didn't know the language and I didn't know a single person to talk to! Upon departure Greg told me that the wife of a fellow soldier was going to come and visit me the next day. I was so excited to meet her and make a new friend. She never showed up. I was heartbroken.

A few days later our Army Chaplain's wife came by for a visit and brought a Hummingbird Cake. (At the time it seemed an unlikely name for a cake. However I soon found out that folklore has it that the hummingbird is a symbol of sweetness. The hummingbird is known to be drawn to intensely sweet sources. They are able to assess the amount of sugar in the nectar they eat. They reject flower types that produce nectar which is less than 12% sugar and prefer those whose sugar content is around 25%.)

My new friend drove me into town, showed me around, and introduced me to other military wives who were in the same spot as I. I hope you can see why this recipe means the world to me and brings back the memory of one of the dearest ladies I have ever met.

P.S. The author of this book, Cathy Horvath, and I recently had lunch at a delightful old home which was turned into the Crabapple Tea Shoppe near Atlanta. It is only open a few hours a day and for lunch only. She and I enjoyed a very nice lunch and then ordered dessert. Can you guess what it was? Hummingbird Cake! This time it was a strawberry cake and it was delectable. There are several variations of the cake, but the basic ingredients are the same.

HUMMINGBIRD CAKE RECIPE ON THE NEXT PAGE

LINDA LAIRD'S HUMMINGBIRD CAKE

INGREDIENTS

3 cups flour

1 1/2 teaspoons vanilla

2 cups sugar

1 teaspoon baking soda

1 teaspoon salt

1 (8oz.) can crushed pineapple

1 teaspoon cinnamon

1 cup chopped pecans

3 eggs, beaten

1 1/2 cups oil

2 cups bananas, chopped

CREAM CHEESE ICING:

1 (8oz.) pkg. cream cheese, softened

1 box powdered sugar

1/2 cup butter (one stick) softened

1 tablespoon vanilla

1/2 cup chopped nuts

PREPARATION

Combine dry ingredients; add eggs and oil. Stir until moist. Do not beat.

Stir in vanilla, pineapple with juice, pecans, and bananas.

Grease and flour 9 x 13 pan. Bake at 350 degrees for 45 to 50 minutes or until it tests done.

Frost with Cream Cheese Icing.

MARIANNE'S PEANUT BUTTER COOKIES

Thanks to my family and friends, I have a reputation for making the best Peanut Butter Cookies. Gary, our fourth child, would ask for these cookies rather than a birthday cake. When my brother Ray was pursuing his education in Europe, he received many care packages containing these cookies. My church and the Arizona Polish Club have sold hundreds of dozens of these cookies for fund raisers over the years. My co-workers were the recipients of my cookies as well. They often said I could make more money selling my cookies than I earned collecting on my accounts! One day our sales secretary even printed me a "license" to sell my cookies on any street corner in Tucson. The story I'm most proud to share concerns a sale of my Peanut Butter Cookies at an AT&T facility in California, while visiting my sons David and Brian.

Marianne Harczak Powell

Brian wanted a double batch of cookie dough, which he helped me mix. The next day I baked them. He took a huge container to work with him in the morning. When he came home for lunch he took the rest. That evening he showed me an email he sent around the office. 'For a donation of $5 or more, you can purchase three Peanut Butter Cookies – the best in the world! (His very words) A free napkin with each sale. All proceeds to go to Katrina Relief.' He raised over $400. He added at the bottom of the email: 'My Mom will cry when she reads this' and of course I did.

David also helped with United Way at AT&T but a different department. His request was that I make the cookies a little larger than usual and put two in plastic wrap. He then sold them at his office and turned in to the United Way hundreds of dollars from the sale of My Mamma's Cookies.

MARIANNE'S PEANUT BUTTER COOKIES RECIPE ON THE NEXT PAGE

MARIANNE'S PEANUT BUTTER COOKIES

INGREDIENTS AND PREPARATION

Combine and beat thoroughly:

1 cup chunky peanut butter

1 cup solid Crisco

1 cup white sugar

1 cup packed brown sugar

1/2 teaspoon salt

1 teaspoon vanilla

When well blended, mix in 2 unbeaten eggs.

Sift 1 1/2 cups flour with 1 teaspoon baking soda. Add to Crisco mixture and blend again. Chill dough.

Measure about 1 teaspoon cookie dough, roll into a ball, and place on greased cookie sheet. Dip a fork into a dish with flour and press lightly into each cookie ball on sheet.

Bake at 325 degrees for 18 to 20 minutes.

Makes about 6 dozen. Store in covered tin or Tupperware.

MARY TODD LINCOLN'S VANILLA ALMOND CAKE

Cathy Horvath

Traditionally, the Senior Class at St. Willibrord High School on the far South Side of Chicago put on an operetta in the spring of each year. In 1956, the nuns decided instead to produce the play "Love is Eternal," the story of Abraham Lincoln and Mary Todd Lincoln. The play was based on the novel by Irving Stone and was about 2 1/2 hours long. When tryouts were announced I auditioned for the part of Ann, Mary's sister. I was absolutely stunned when the lead parts were announced over the loudspeaker system during one of my classes. I had the lead. Later it was decided that the part should be played by two different students, each taking one night's performance. My group of "actors" covered the first performance. It was quite a challenge to remember all those lines because Mary was on stage most of the time. The play ended with a dramatic scene between Mary and President Lincoln. We were given a standing ovation, and someone presented me with a gorgeous presentation bouquet of red roses. The card had no signature; just a lovely congratulatory note. What a high! Many years later I've come across several of Mary Todd Lincoln's favorite recipes while living in the White House. Here's one of them:

MARY TODD LINCOLN'S VANILLA ALMOND CAKE RECIPE ON THE NEXT PAGE

MARY TODD LINCOLN'S VANILLA ALMOND CAKE

INGREDIENTS

1 1/2 cups sugar

1 cup butter

1 teaspoon vanilla

2 3/4 cups sifted cake flour

1 teaspoon baking powder

1 1/3 cups milk

1 cup almonds, finely chopped

6 egg whites, beaten until stiff

WHITE FROSTING

1 cup sugar

1/3 cup water

1/4 teaspoon cream of tartar

1 dash salt

2 egg whites

1 teaspoon vanilla

PREPARATION

Cream together sugar, butter and vanilla. Stir together the cake flour and baking powder; add to creamed mixture alternately with milk. Stir in almonds. Gently fold in the egg whites. Pour into two greased and lightly floured 9 inch round baking pans. Bake at 375 degrees for 28 to 30 minutes. Cool 10 minutes; remove from pans. Fill and frost with White Frosting.

WHITE FROSTING

In a saucepan combine sugar, water, cream of tartar and salt. Bring mixture to boiling, stirring until the sugar dissolves.

Place egg whites in a mixing bowl; very slowly pour the hot sugar syrup over, beating constantly with electric mixer until stiff peaks form, about 7 minutes. Beat in vanilla.

MARYLAND CRAB CAKES

When I was 14 years old my family moved from Pawnee City, NE to Baltimore, MD in 1943, where my mother helped build B-26 war planes and my step-father helped build Liberty ships. One of the highlights in my memory was the crab cakes served in that city. They were as common on menus as hamburgers, and oh, how delicious. I accompanied my uncle as he made his rounds repairing refrigeration equipment, and those crab cakes were such a welcome and fragrant aroma… and taste treat.

Richard Morgan

MARYLAND
CRAB
CAKES

INGREDIENTS

1 pound fresh domestic, lump or back fin blue crab meat, picked over to remove any shells

1 egg, beaten

1/4 cup Hellman's mayonnaise

1 teaspoon dry mustard

1 teaspoon Old Bay seasoning

1/4 teaspoon cayenne pepper

1/4 cup chopped parsley

2 teaspoons Worcestershire sauce

1/2 teaspoon Tabasco sauce or to taste

4 slices thin Pepperidge Farm white bread

Finely crushed saltines (enough to coat crab cakes)

PREPARATION

Remove crusts from bread. Cut in small cubes. Place on baking sheet in 300 degree oven until cubes begin to dry.

In a large bowl, mix mayonnaise, mustard, beaten egg, Old Bay, Worcestershire, Tabasco, cayenne and parsley. Fold in bread. Fold in crab meat.

Line a cookie sheet with waxed paper. After shaping each cake (makes about 8 crab cakes), dust each side with finely crushed saltines and place on waxed paper. Cover with plastic wrap and put in fridge for an hour or so before frying, baking or broiling.

If frying, fry in 50/50 mix of butter/vegetable oil at medium heat. Don't scorch.

MICHAEL'S TEDDY BEAR BREAD

Joan is my husband's cousin. We have always had an ongoing mutual admiration for each other because we have the same values. Family comes first in our lives. Joan is an incredible cook and

Joan

although I have many talents, her culinary expertise is far beyond mine. Like most of us, she has experienced some tough times in her life, but nothing prepared her for the death of her little boy. Michael will always be remembered in our hearts and our prayers. This is Joan's story and recipe:

"By profession, I am a high school English teacher, but in my heart of hearts, I am foremost a mom. Nothing matters to me more than my children, so when I decided to temporarily give up my career to be a stay-at-home mom, no one was surprised. My daughter, Vicki, and my son, Michael, were convinced that being a mom meant baking goodies and giving hugs and kisses.

One morning, when Michael was about 2 1/2 years old, he was snuggled up in my lap while I was recipe searching through magazines. Suddenly his eyes lit up, he stuck his finger into a page and said, 'Mom, I want that teddy bear!' I tried to explain that the teddy bear was only a loaf of bread. He said, 'No problem, Mommy. Make it for me. You can do it!' Needless to say, this early in my culinary experience, the task seemed daunting, but my son's confidence in my ability spurred me on. I tackled the recipe, amended the recipe, changed a few minor ingredients and, much to Michael's delight, created several, successful teddy bear loaves.

Today, almost 30 years later, 'Teddy' is very much a part of my baking repertoire. He makes appearances at baby showers, christenings, children's birthdays and many other family functions. He's been ribboned, decorated and dressed to celebrate many special occasions.

Michael passed away at age 3 1/2 from complications that arose during surgery, just one short year after requesting his very first, special Teddy. I know in my heart that wherever Teddy makes an appearance these days, Michael is smiling down from the Heavens and saying, 'Thank you, Mommy. I knew you could do it!'"

MICHAEL'S TEDDY BEAR BREAD RECIPE ON THE NEXT PAGE

TEDDY BEAR BREAD

(makes two)

INGREDIENTS

1/2 cup milk

3 tablespoons sugar

2 teaspoons salt

3 tablespoons margarine

2 pkgs. active dry yeast

1 1/2 cups warm water

6 1/2 - 7 cups unsifted,
all purpose flour

1 egg beaten with
1 tablespoon water

6 raisins

PREPARATION

Heat milk, water, sugar, salt and margarine over low heat to 120° (on candy thermometer). In large bowl, mix 3 cups flour with yeast. Add warm milk mixture. Beat until smooth. Stir in enough remaining flour to make a fairly stiff (not sticky) dough. Knead 8-10 minutes. Place in a greased bowl. Turn over to grease top. Cover bowl with plastic wrap and a blanket, and let dough rise until doubled in size (usually 1 - 1 1/2 hours). Punch dough down and divide into four equal parts.

Leave two parts undivided. Divide the third part in half and divide the fourth part into 14 equal pieces. Shape all parts into round balls. Place the two large balls on two separate greased cookie sheets. These will be the bears' bodies. Place medium balls above the bodies (touching the bodies) for bears' heads. Flatten slightly. Attach 14 small balls to bodies for ears, hands, feet and noses. Cover. Let rise until doubled (about 45 minutes). Press slightly to indent ears. Place raisins for eyes and belly buttons (push in a bit). Brush entire bodies with the one egg that has been beaten with 1 tablespoon water.

Bake at 375° for about 30 minutes. Cool completely. Move carefully to plate so as not to dislodge arms or legs.

MITSY'S LIFE EXPERIENCE

In 1999, I started working for Smith Barney, a national brokerage firm. At that time I was the only female broker among fifty brokers. In front of my office sat a beautiful black woman named Diane, a sales assistant for another broker. She was very private and I later found out she was 60 years old. I decided to make small talk for a while but could tell she had no interest. I assumed she chose not to talk because there was no benefit from talking to me. I didn't pay her salary.

Women in the financial consulting industry are very competitive. The fact that I was the only woman in production in our office and that she worked for another broker, put us on opposing teams so to speak.

About six months into my job, I walked into the office wearing a blouse that she said was identical to one she owned a year earlier. She proceeded to tell me how she loved that blouse but, unfortunately, the office shredder caught the front of it one day and shredded quite a bit of it before she could turn the machine off. I thought that was funny and just kept going with her story and she began laughing hysterically at me laughing at her. That was the beginning of a beautiful relationship and one that started with "laughter is the best medicine".

Despite the twenty years' difference in our ages, we became very good friends. Diane also befriended my mother who was only a few years older than she. Diane called herself my Black Mother and my real Mom was just Mom. There were several times when we three were shopping together and I would say "Mom" and both women would turn around and look at me. Folks around us would look at us as if thinking "WOW that's a progressive family; way ahead of their time."

Diane finally started opening up to me about her personal life and I realized that she had lost a daughter who would have been my age. Her daughter had a kidney transplant and only lived for two years longer. She passed away due to other complications. On top of that Diane was a thirteen year breast cancer survivor and was the face of breast cancer on many hospital brochures.

In 2004 I left Smith Barney but Diane and I remained good friends and often met for lunch. One day I called her office and was informed that she had been admitted to the hospital. I tracked her down at Crawford Long Hospital and when I walked in the room she began crying. She said "there is my little angel." She told me she had a rare uterine cancer and was undergoing treatment. Tears welled up in my eyes but she told me that whatever I did, I couldn't cry because she needed me to be strong.

She returned to work but only for a short time. The chemotherapy tired her too much. When I visited her at her home, her life partner, Ed, would cook nice lunches for us. I planted things in her garden while she watched and smiled. Many months later, she went back into the hospital. On July 2, 2005, my mom and I went to visit her and told her that we would bring her barbecue on the 4th. She said "I may not be able to eat ribs but I sure would like to suck the bones." We all had a good laugh. On July 4th, we went to visit and Diane had had a stroke and was no longer able to speak. I had to walk out of her room quickly because I knew I couldn't cry. My mom and I told Ed to leave and get some rest while we sat with Diane for hours. Diane's kidneys began to fail.

As her body began to shut down, I had the pleasure of meeting her entire family. Using the word pleasure sounds strange, I know, but they were a gift to my life. Somewhat of a routine set it. Every day I would spend my lunch hour with her. After 4:00 P.M. I would return and stay with her and her family until 10:00 P.M. On July 10th, I left work early and went to visit Diane. When I entered her hospital room and

she saw me, she made a really strange sigh. Her family said she had a really rough day. Ed told her that she could leave this earth and it was ok, but he also let her know that I would be there at 4:15.

Diane had an Aunt whom they called a prayer warrior. When it came time for Diane to leave this earth, her Aunt asked that we all wrap around the bed and pray for a peaceful departure for her. I was the only white person in the room and while in that circle, the Aunt thanked me. She told me that Diane had spoken of me often. She shared with me that through our friendship, Diane had learned that regardless of our color, our blood runs red and that our souls were the same color. I stood with them in that room and saw and heard Diane take her last breath. I feel like I saw Diane's soul leave her body but just in case, I went out in the hall to cry. I still wanted to be strong in case she was still in the room.

I grew up that day and any prejudice I may have ever had left me with Diane's soul. I was invited to the wake and the funeral. Afterwards, Ed gave me a tiny urn of Diane's ashes. I have remained friends with Ed and Diane's family. I thank God for sending Diane into my life.

MOLLY ALEXANDER DARDEN

In August of 1979 I decided that I wanted to begin a professional writing career. I knew the competition would be stiff, but I hoped that my degree in English would help me land a job at our local daily newspaper *The Lakeland Ledger*. Once there, I could start making contacts so that I could find a way to progress. My previous experience included being a Spanish interpreter and administrative assistant.

"Proofreading was the most appropriate job available," said the Human Resources person. I began my editorial career by scouring editorials and advertisements, looking for words misused or misspelled. When the lead editorial submitted the word, auger (a carpenter's tool), I knew it should be augur (to predict by signs or omens). After some back-and-forth with the Executive Editor, we brought out the dictionary. Ah HAH! Augur: It would augur well…" I had caught his attention and respect.

Gathering courage to approach the Managing Editor (ME), I presented my application. With a laugh bordering on a sneer, he immediately told me no openings were available for copy editors. Whether he didn't like my looks, didn't like women, or just couldn't stomach bringing a proofreader from the bowels of the paper in to the hallowed newsroom, I really didn't care. I was qualified, and I was determined to get a fair opportunity to at least try out for the job.

When the opportunity presented itself to meet with the Publisher, I presented my case and my application to him. He agreed to give me a 5-day trial on the copy desk – after my usual shift downstairs. That meant breaking into a new field for me, and I didn't care how hard I had to work to get it; in the long run, it would certainly be worth it.

The ME introduced me to the News Editor, who told me what he expected me to do: write headlines!! I also had to remove chunks of the stories we received from the Associated Press and other wire services, so that the content still read seamlessly and all important information was included. The work was exhilarating, though daunting, and I loved it.

They hired me and assigned me to run the Religion section in addition to editing the news stories and writing headlines. After eighteen months we parted company, and I went on to edit a community newspaper.

Looking back, if I could do it over I would learn to be more politically-savvy in order to better negotiate the behind-the-scenes machinations that would have solidified my position. My experience at The Ledger has strengthened me so that I'm now "gender-blind." In work situations I see myself without gender, judged on my merits, and that has enabled me to move forward, gaining respect and strength as I go. Of course, I work hard to maintain my standard of excellence, but I'm judged by my performance and knowledge, and that's as it should be.

MOM'S BEANS AND SAUSAGE

We always had a large gathering of family and friends for special occasions such as graduations. I did most of the cooking and prepared Mostacolli, ham, potato salad, Jell-O molds, bean salad—you know, the usual party fare. Mom came up with this recipe to accompany grilled Italian sausage and it soon became a favorite. Hope it will be among yours too. It's easy but so delicious.

Cathy Horvath

MOM'S
BEANS AND
SAUSAGE

INGREDIENTS

1 lb. pinto beans

1 lb. Italian sausage cut into 2 inch pieces

1 6oz. can tomato paste

1 8oz. can pizza sauce

1 14.5oz. can tomatoes

1 teaspoon oregano

PREPARATION

Soak beans overnight then boil until they are slightly cooked. Drain beans; set water aside. Fry sausage pieces until lightly browned. When sausage is lightly cooked remove from pan.

Blend tomato paste, pizza sauce, tomatoes and oregano together in a bowl. Place beans in a large pot, add sausage, tomato mixture and enough saved water to cover. Cook on low heat for about an hour, adding more saved water if necessary. Consistency is thick when done.

MOM'S CHRISTMAS ICE BOX CAKE

"Aunt Marge" holds a special place in my family's heart, even though she passed away a long time ago. Diane is one of her two daughters. They both exude their Mom's sweetness and thoughtfulness. It is my honor to present Diane's memory and

Diane Dailey Finney

her Mom's recipe. She writes:

"This is my Mom's recipe that she made only for Christmas. It is very rich and was very expensive for her to make. That is why she made it just for her favorite holiday. We were so excited to get one piece each but it was worth the wait."

MOM'S
CHRISTMAS
ICE BOX CAKE

INGREDIENTS

2 dozen vanilla wafers

4 bars German Sweet Chocolate (1 lb.total)

5 tablespoons hot water

4 tablespoons powdered sugar

8 eggs, separated

1 teaspoon vanilla

PREPARATION

In a medium size pan, over medium heat, place chocolate, hot water & powdered sugar. Stir well. After all is melted, remove from heat and add egg yolks one at a time. Beat well after each egg yolk is added. Beat egg whites until they form a peak. Fold into chocolate mixture and add vanilla. Line a 9 x 13 glass pan with vanilla wafers (sides and bottom). Crush some of the cookies to fill in spaces on the bottom of the pan. Pour half of the chocolate mixture into the pan. Place a layer of vanilla wafers on the chocolate mixture. Cover with the remaining chocolate mixture. Let stand overnight. Garnish with whipping cream and enjoy!

MOM'S MINESTRONE

When I was growing up, most Moms had their own recipe for homemade soup. Usually, the ingredients depended on what was left in the refrigerator and pantry. There's nothing better on a cold rainy day than to sit down to a bowl of hot soup, warm bread lathered in butter, and a tossed salad. That was a complete meal.

Cathy Horvath

One of our family's favorite was Minestrone. There are as many recipes for Minestrone as there are for Spaghetti Sauce. Whether homemade, served in a restaurant, or from a can, no two soups are alike. This is the recipe my mom wrote down for me shortly after I was married in 1959. The recipe card is somewhat faded and messy now, but I refuse to rewrite it. It was Mom's original, after all.

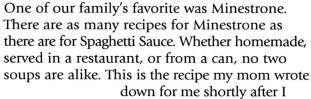

MOM'S
MINESTRONE

INGREDIENTS

1 lb. dry pinto beans

2 stalks celery, chopped

3 potatoes, peeled and cubed

2 carrots, sliced

1 onion, chopped

1/4 head cabbage, shredded

1 palmful barley or lentils or both

1 clove garlic, minced

1 teaspoon dried basil leaves

1 teaspoon marjoram

1 teaspoon thyme

1 package small pasta like pennette, ditalini, etc.

grated Parmesan cheese

SOFFRITTO: *(thickening agent or soup base)*

1 tablespoon butter and 1 tablespoon olive oil

1/2 finely chopped onion

1 clove garlic, minced

2 tablespoons tomato paste

1/2 cup water

Salt and pepper to taste

PREPARATION

Rinse beans in cold water, drain, and soak overnight in a large kettle with enough water to cover beans. In the morning, drain the beans and add enough cold water until the kettle is a little over 3/4 full (about 4 quarts). Add salt to taste. Cook over medium high heat. In the meantime, cut up vegetables. When beans start to boil, add vegetables, herbs, barley, and lentils. Slow boil for two hours. During this time just before adding the noodles, make the base: melt butter and oil; add onions, garlic, and tomato paste mixed with water, salt and pepper. Simmer until onions are soft and golden. Add more water if needed.

Add base to soup, stirring well. Add noodles and continue cooking until noodles are done. If the soup gets too thick just add water or vegetable stock.

Serve with freshly grated Parmesan cheese sprinkled over the soup.

MOM'S STUFATO (Stew) AND POLENTA

I have to giggle to myself when an old family recipe that was a meal stretcher becomes a "new" culinary dish. The same can be said for risotto. Nonetheless, it is in my Mom's honor that I present this family favorite. My Dad used to make a big deal out of making the Polenta. He would stir the cornmeal for over an hour with a huge wooden spoon and then pour it out on a breadboard and set it on the porch to firm up. Not necessary. The recipe that follows works just fine.

Cathy Horvath

STUFATO
AND
POLENTA

INGREDIENTS STUFATO

1-2 lbs. beef stew meat

1 cup chopped onions

Salt and pepper to taste

Dash allspice

2 leaves of thyme

3/4 cup chopped celery

1 8 ounce can tomato sauce

1 cup beef broth or more to taste

1/2 bag frozen peas or green beans

3 - 4 medium size potatoes, peeled and cut into 2 inch chunks

6 carrots, peeled and slices into 1 inch pieces

INGREDIENTS POLENTA

6 cups water

2 teaspoons salt

1 3/4 cups yellow cornmeal

3 tablespoons unsalted butter

3/4 cup grated Parmesan cheese

PREPARATION STUFATO

Brown meat in small amount of corn oil with onions and spices. Add tomato sauce and broth. Simmer for 30 minutes. Add vegetables and more broth to cover ingredients. Simmer for an additional 30 minutes or until all ingredients are cooked. Serve over polenta.

PREPARATION POLENTA

Boil the water in a large saucepan. Add the salt. Gradually whisk in the cornmeal. (It will lump if you don't add it slowly.) Lower the heat and cook, stirring often, until the mixture thickens and the cornmeal is tender. (About 15 minutes) Remove the pan from the heat and add butter and the cheese. Stir until all is melted. Pour into a glass baking pan or dish and set aside to cool for a few minutes. It will firm up as it does so. Then place a large helping on each plate and cover with the stew.

My Mom used to refrigerate the left over polenta and the next day would cut into squares and toast in the oven. It will be really firm then and serves as a nice side dish.

MRS. HORVATH'S CHINA

Cathy Horvath

When my husband, Ray, and his brother, Ernie, were in the Air Force stationed overseas in the 1950's, they bought my mother-in-law all the components to set a gorgeous table. Ray purchased a complete set of Rosenthal China in the Aida pattern because she loved orchids. The pattern is a lovely design of pale mauve and lavender orchids; the pieces are trimmed in gold. Ray bought every piece that Rosenthal manufactured, from teapot to cracker tray. He also bought a matching set of crystal with the orchid pattern beautifully etched on each piece—from sherbet glass to champagne flute.

To accompany that, his brother bought his mom a sterling silver coffee and tea service with a matching serving tray. All that was missing was the sterling flatware. So my father-in-law bought that here in the States. Mrs. Horvath had a lovely mahogany dining room set in her new home, and was well prepared to entertain in style. She was a classy lady and loved beautiful things. She used her new possessions only once or twice in over 25 years because she considered it much too precious to use more often.

My parents in law are deceased now and I have inherited their beautiful china and crystal—or what's left of it. You see, when they were seriously ill they each had a nursing service that cared for them around the clock in their home. They promised each other that neither would send the other to a nursing home as their lives neared the end. The china and crystal were used as every day dishes and were subsequently cracked and chipped or destroyed all together. What is left I gave to my daughter Jenny and we have been filling in the missing pieces through a china replacement service ever since. Jenny cherishes her Grandmother's pieces and has since set an exquisite table for her dinner guests on several occasions. She has modernized the dishes using charger plates in a complementary color. It looks beautiful! I'm sure Mrs. H is very proud.

I agree with my mother-in-law in using my finer things for special occasions only. For me, special occasions include birthdays, anniversaries, and holidays, the first day of Spring, the first report card with straight A's, the first touch down, the birth of the first grandchild — you get the idea. If you don't, someone else will long after you pass away, so what did that accomplish? From what I have read and heard, using your good china and silver only enhances their beauty. So go ahead and enjoy your treasures!

MRS. HORVATH'S STUFFED CABBAGE

When I was a new bride, I wanted to please my husband by learning to cook the recipes his mother made. Coming from an Italian background, I was embarking on a totally new culinary adventure because Ray is Hungarian. I have since come to realize that there are as many versions of stuffed cabbage as there are for spaghetti sauce, but I prefer Mrs. Horvath's version and have never changed it.

Cathy Horvath

MRS. HORVATH'S
STUFFED
CABBAGE

INGREDIENTS

3/4 lb. ground pork

3/4 lb. ground beef

2 teaspoons salt

1 teaspoon paprika

1/2 teaspoon black pepper

3 cups cooked rice

1 medium onion, minced or 2 tablespoon dried minced onions

1 egg

2 large heads of cabbage

1 8 ounce can tomato sauce

2-3 tablespoons butter cut into 1 inch slices

PREPARATION

Core cabbage and place in enough boiling water to cover. With a fork in one hand and a knife in the other, keep pulling off the leaves as they become wilted. Drain well. Mix the first eight ingredients until well blended. Place about 3-4 tablespoons of mixture on top of each cabbage leaf. Depending on the size of the leaf you may add more or less. Then roll the leaf, tucking in the ends with your fingers. Place the stuffed leaves seam side down in a Dutch oven and add tomato sauce and enough water to cover. If you wind up with a lot of cabbage rolls, additional tomato sauce can be added. Top with a few small slices of butter if desired. Bake at 350 degrees for about an hour.

NEW ORLEANS RED BEANS & RICE

Sandra Morgan, my dear friend of many years, is a gorgeous, truly Southern lady. She has a natural talent for cooking that I envy. She and her husband Richard have the knack of creating something wonderful out of whatever is in the kitchen cupboards. This is one of her favorite recipes:

Sandra Morgan

"When I was a girl growing up in New Orleans, everybody had Red Beans & Rice for lunch or dinner every Monday! Monday being wash day, and wash day requiring a lot of attention, wives/ women made Red Beans and Rice because it didn't need much tending. It was put in an old iron pot early in the cool of the morning and left to cook for the rest of the day. You could walk down the street or along an alley and smell them cooking…open windows and no air conditioning…so the aroma wafted easily.

One of my first paying jobs was in the Records Library at Charity Hospital in New Orleans. Would you believe, on Mondays, even the patients were served Red Beans & Rice?!

After high school graduation I got a job with an oil company, and went "out" to lunch and on Mondays, on the menus in restaurants could be found Red Beans & Rice. Whether you were in the hospital or at the Monteleone Hotel, Red Beans & Rice was served. Even today in popular, familiar and famous restaurants, this "soul food" is on the menus on Mondays. So at least once a week, in New Orleans, everybody was and still is "in the same pot"!

NEW ORLEANS RED BEANS & RICE RECIPE ON THE NEXT PAGE

NEW ORLEANS
RED BEANS
& RICE

INGREDIENTS

1 lb dried red kidney beans

1/4 cup chopped celery

1 quart water

1/2 teaspoon Tabasco

1 ham bone with ham

Salt and pepper to taste

1 large onion, chopped

1 bay leaf

1/4 teaspoon thyme

2 cloves garlic, minced

3 cups hot cooked rice

PREPARATION

Place beans on a cookie sheet and pick over for broken beans or debris.

Soak beans overnight in pot of water. When ready to cook the next day, in a large heavy pan or Dutch Oven, sauté ham with the onion and garlic just until the vegetables are transparent. Add remaining ingredients except rice (be sure to drain the beans after the overnight soaking). Simmer 3 hours or until beans are tender. Add water when necessary during cooking. Water should barely cover beans at end of cooking time.

When the beans are done, remove ham bone, cut off meat and add to beans. Remove 1 cup of beans and mash or puree in blender. Add to beans and stir until liquid is thickened. Adjust seasonings. Serve hot over white rice.

Serves 6

NO BAKE COOKIES

Have your kids ever approached you at 9 o'clock at night to say they need to bring a treat to school? Or hear from a member of the church group calling to apologize for the last minute request for a contribution to the bake sale? Or you just remembered you are supposed to bring something to the farewell luncheon for a member of your office? Fear not! This recipe is the solution. There's every likelihood that you already have the ingredients in your cabinets.

Chris Horvath

P.S. When there are no snacks in our house, our son, Chris, likes to whip up a batch of these goodies because they're quick and delicious.

NO BAKE
COOKIES

INGREDIENTS

2 cups sugar

1/2 cup cocoa

1 stick butter

1/2 cup milk

1/2 cup peanut butter—chunky is the best!

1 teaspoon vanilla

2 1/2 cups regular oatmeal

PREPARATION

Mix and bring to a boil the first 4 ingredients. Boil for 2 minutes.

Remove from heat and let cool for 1 minute.

Add peanut butter and stir until melted. Add vanilla and oatmeal.

Stir and drop from teaspoon onto wax paper and let harden.

NONNA'S FIORI di ZUCCA

Typing this recipe brings back a lot of memories for me. Nonna (Grandmother in Italian) tended a vegetable garden ever since I can remember. Included in the grand selection of vegetables

Cathy Horvath

were zucchini plants. As were all Italian gardeners and cooks of her time, Nonna was good at making a variety of dishes with the prolific plants. When my husband and I moved from the city to the suburbs of Chicago, one of the first things we did was plant a garden. The better the success one year, the bigger the garden the next. And so it grew from a tiny plot to a "plantation" 30 feet x 25 feet. Besides the standard lettuce and tomatoes, we tried sweet corn, radishes, beans, carrots, asparagus, cucumbers, potatoes, and strawberries. Some species worked well and produced a good harvest; others were a bust. Each year we always planted and grew zucchini.

There are so many ways to prepare zucchini, but the most fun is cooking the blossoms. That's right; this recipe is for fried zucchini blossoms. When I made them for my children and their friends, I wouldn't tell them what they were eating until they tasted the blossoms. To a child, they would say how delicious whatever they were eating was and when I told them that they had just eaten a flower, they were blown away! But they came back for seconds and thirds. Hope you enjoy this recipe as much as I always did as a child waiting for my Nonna to return from her garden with an apron full of the blossoms. By the way, if you can't buy them,

and wish to plant the zucchini in your garden, it is best to pluck the blossom from the mature plant early in the morning when they are open and easier to clean.

NONNA'S
FIORI
DI ZUCCA

INGREDIENTS

25 zucchini blossoms
1 stick unsalted butter, or 1/2 cup olive oil
flour
4 well beaten eggs
Salt and pepper to taste

PREPARATION

Open the centers of the flowers gently. Remove the pistils and stigmas, and discard. Wash the flowers under running water and carefully dry them on a paper towel. Place each blossom in the flour and then roll gently in the eggs. Fry them in melted butter or olive oil in a frying pan over medium heat until golden, about 2 to 3 minutes, turning several times so they are evenly browned. Remove when they are still firm. Drain on brown paper to absorb excess butter or oil, then sprinkle with salt and pepper.

NONNA'S GARDINIERA

My Italian Grandmother (Nonna) and Grandfather (Nonno) labored every day in their huge Victory Garden located in an open field on the far south side of Chicago. In the neighborhood called Pullman, most folks took a plot of that field and planted their gardens. I can still see my grandparents bent over their crops-- planting, raking and pulling weeds. The war against weeds never ended. They harvested wonderful fresh vegetables that they either ate in the spring or summer months or preserved for the cold months ahead. One of the products from their garden was an assortment of vegetables that were marinated in a brine and kept in a tall apothecary jar or in canning jars. It's called Giardiniera and can be purchased at most grocery stores today if you choose not to follow this recipe. It makes a great addition to an antipasto tray.

Cathy Horvath

When I was a toddler, my mother and I paid a visit to Nonna in the kitchen of her row house apartment on Corliss Avenue. We sat at the table that I remember as being white porcelain trimmed in red. My Grandmother let me choose a small pearl onion to eat from the apothecary jar of vegetables because that was my favorite. I savored the vinegary juice from the tiny onion. But when I swallowed it, the onion got lodged in my throat and I began to choke. The frantic women patted my back really hard but it wouldn't dislodge! I kept choking! Then they held me upside down while they patted even harder. As my body swung from the hard pats, I hit my head on the kitchen table and the onion popped out of my mouth! If only they knew the Heimlich maneuver back then, it probably would've been a less traumatic experience for us all! This is a nice recipe—just don't serve it to toddlers!

NONNA'S
GARDINIERA
RECIPE
ON THE
NEXT PAGE

GARDINIERA (PICKLED VEGETABLES)

INGREDIENTS

1 large cauliflower head cut into flowerets (1 1/2 inches)

1 lb. carrots cut in coins

1/2 to 1 lb. pearl onions

2 cups celery cut into 1/4 inch pieces

6 garlic cloves

2 bell peppers, red and yellow, cut into 1inch strips

1 cup non-iodized salt

4 quarts cold water

2 quarts white vinegar

1/4 cup mustard seed

2 tablespoons celery seed

1/2 teaspoon red pepper flakes

2 1/2 cups sugar

PREPARATION:

Prepare vegetables. Dissolve the salt in cold water in a large bowl. Add vegetables, cover and refrigerate for 12 to 18 hours. Then drain vegetables, rinse them in cold water, and drain again.

Combine vinegar, mustard seed, celery seed, and sugar in a stainless steel or enamel pan. Bring to a boil and continue boiling for 3 minutes. Add vegetables, reduce heat and cook uncovered, until vegetables are almost tender (about 5 -10 minutes) – do not overcook as the vegetables will be soggy.

Fill hot pint canning jars, wipe rims with a damp cloth, screw on lids and set aside to cool. Test the seal by pressing down on the lid with your finger. If the lid stays down, the jar is properly sealed. If not, store the contents in the refrigerator.

Store the rest of the jars in a cool dry place.

OMELETS IN A BAG

Vicki is a friend I met shortly after moving to the Atlanta area. She is creative, kind and sweet. It is no wonder she would come up with a most unusual contribution to this book. She writes:

Vicki

"Every year I do a Christmas letter and it includes a favorite recipe from that year. The following recipe got the most feedback. I heard back from many to say that they used this recipe when large family gatherings took place. It was a form of entertainment too, and even the kids like to participate and create their own. A good friend teaches a college marketing course and uses this recipe as a team building exercise. Her students are sure it won't work, but are delighted when it does. When she needs an attention getting introduction, she also uses this recipe and relates it back to marketing. It is quite amazing and oh so simple."

OMELETS
IN A
BAG

INGREDIENTS AND PREPARATION

- Have guests write their name on a quart-size freezer bag with permanent marker.

- Crack 2 eggs (large or extra-large) into the bag (not more than 2) shake to combine them.

- Put out a variety of ingredients such as: cheeses, ham, onion, green pepper, tomato, hash browns, salsa, etc.

- Each guest adds prepared ingredients of choice to their bag and shakes. Make sure to get the air out of the bag and zip it up.

- Place the bags into rolling, boiling water for exactly 13 minutes. You can usually cook 6-8 omelets in a large pot. For more, make another pot of boiling water.

- Open the bags and the omelet will roll out easily.

Nice to serve with fresh fruit and coffee cake: everyone gets involved in the preparation and it is a great conversation piece.

ONLY YOU ARE IN CONTROL

Only you are in control of yourself—no one else. My best friend, Joan, realized that after living through the death of her daughter and many hours of therapy.

Joan Kesman

Her lesson came with two years of helping her daughter, Kerry, the second of four daughters, fight her battle with leukemia. Kerry was an attractive, intelligent young woman in her late twenties who was diagnosed shortly after she was married. She and her husband lived in the Dallas area, and Joan and her family lived in the Hinsdale, IL. area (a suburb of Chicago.) Kerry was busy with her career in window dressing for designer retail stores. Joan worked long hours at her beauty salon. Joan struggled to be with her daughter as frequently as she would have liked. They spoke often and Kerry flew home to Hinsdale to visit every so often.

But Joan, being Joan, was not about to accept Kerry's diagnosis as a death warrant. Joan researched and read anything she could get her hands on. She embarked on a mission to locate a healing modality for her daughter. This was back in the early 1990's; there wasn't much to go on. However, Joan is a strong proponent for alternative medicine. Her search for a healing took many directions. She read copious books and talked with many people who gave her new places to search.

Kerry was a willing participant in several healing methodologies, but to no avail. They tried healers, supplements, intravenous herbal liquids, but nothing had a lasting impact on her health. There was one last hope—Joan had read about the successes of a cancer clinic in Mexico and strongly urged Kerry to give it a try. Much to Joan's distress, Kerry said no. Who knows why? Maybe she was tired of trying. She was still very sick and getting worse each day. Her body was giving out. Her blood count was not good and the doctors told her that she needed a bone marrow transplant. She opted for it even though Joan was against it and wanted her to go to Mexico.

The preparation for the bone marrow transplant from her sister made her very sick and it was a horrible experience to watch her suffer. The medical staff gave her tremendous doses of radiation. Kerry lasted three months. She died at twenty nine years of age in January, 1993. Perhaps at some level she knew it was time for her to leave this place and return to her Heavenly Home. We all have a timeline for that, but we're not consciously aware of it.

Joan has spent many hours rethinking those years, meditating, and praying. Sometimes she hears Kerry speaking to her, assuring her that she is very happy, and has a head of beautiful long hair that she lost from the cancer. Joan's lesson: Kerry was in charge of Kerry. She and she alone could make the final decision for her life. Kerry was in charge of Kerry's life, not her mother. Painful as that is to accept, Joan realizes that now and is at peace.

We can't make decisions for others; in the end, we each have to answer for ourselves.

However, we can offer suggestions or recommendations based on our knowledge and experience after asking if our input is wanted. More often than not, people just want someone to listen and to care.

OPEN MIND, CLOSED MOUTH

Cathy Horvath

I don't know where I heard or read that phrase "open mind, closed mouth," – or who mentioned it to me in passing, but I have used it as a guideline in my role as a mother-in-law. Anyone who has been on the receiving end of criticism while doing their best to parent, to be a wife or husband and provider will understand how deeply the criticism can hurt. While we all can do with a few how-to lessons now and then, I have found it advantageous to keep my opinions to myself.

My mom was good at that. She was a big help during the years my children were babies and toddlers. The teenage years were a different matter. Of our four children, two were boys; she and my dad had three girls. She was always supportive and tried to be helpful, even though there were times she couldn't relate to the issues with which I was dealing. She would just say: "I'll pray for you." Dad was a different story. He always had an opinion. He was a very smart man and many times he was right. Many times, but not always. He would judge me and point out my inadequacies, but he never knew the full scope of what was going on or had occurred. He only saw things from his angle and he didn't live with us on a daily basis, so he couldn't possibly have seen the whole picture. What's worse, he didn't

even try. A perfect example was when he told me that the only problem my mentally ill son had was that he just needed someone to talk to like him, his grandpa. My polite response was to ask if the family counselors, psychologists, psychiatrists, parents, and siblings weren't enough. I remember how that conversation felt and remind myself of that from time to time. It's funny how we don't forget a hurt. I don't want that for my children.

Uninformed criticism taught me a great lesson. My children's parenting styles are very different from mine, but it's their style and their children. Who is to say what is right? Their handling of finances is different in many ways from the way I would handle them. Who is to say which method is correct? Some of the choices they make would not be mine. Who is to say I'm right and they're wrong? When asked for advice, I give it with the best of intentions. That's the operative word here INTENTIONS. I want to impart the benefit of my life experiences to help them avoid the same pitfalls. And when they ask for help and I give it, they are grateful. Sometimes they are impressed with what I know or that I've experienced the same thing. Most important of all is that they respect me and take to heart what I have to say because they know I come from a place of unconditional love and want only to help.

The big lesson here for me is to keep my mouth shut. That is the hard part. Believe me! I have to remind myself that they are on their own individual life path and through experience they learn. I have to catch myself every now and then because it would be so easy to say something. For example, I really wanted to tie into my former son-in-law for the misery he put my daughter through when they lost their home and business to bankruptcy. He made many bad business decisions that cost them their business, their home and even their little toddlers' toys. Everything had to go. He stole my daughter's spirit and it has taken many years to see the sparkle in her eyes return. But I said nothing. Their problems were theirs to resolve. It would

have been so easy to let him know how I felt, but I'm glad I didn't. They have since divorced and I see him every now and then when he picks up my granddaughters for "his weekend." For my granddaughters' sake I am glad I have remained silent. Had I not, it would have made for a very awkward relationship among us all. He and my daughter have a civil relationship for the sake of the girls and my husband and I support that. That's as it should be.

I have a daughter-in-law too. I know she loves and respects me, but I only give advice when asked—and she does from time to time. I think we both like it that way! She doesn't know it, but I consider it a compliment that she calls upon me—even if it's to clarify a baking problem. I feel blessed when that happens.

POT LUCK WEDDING

While planning our recent nuptials (we have been together for 10 years, so this came as quite a surprise to many) I had visions of Martha Stewart-esqe elegance. I "saw" how I would effortlessly prepare 14 centerpieces, bake a Strata, roast asparagus as well as throw together gluten free muffins for 40 while making the perfect Spinach salad, and mixing Bellini's, all while spinning plates like a flying Wallenda in a veritable orgy of pre-wedding preparation. Whew! Get the picture?

Suzanne Mark
The (pot) LUCKiest
girl on the planet

Too gradually, I noticed that my VISION of what was to be was a BIT grander than my ability to carry the vision out. Simply put, I was over-achieving. Then came the not-so- subtle suggestion of my personal muse/friend, Lila, who said, 'YOU ARE NOT COOKING FOR YOUR WEDDING!' She sagely advised that we do a Pot Luck Wedding. 'Potluck wedding? I blanched. WHAT?!'

OK, I might as well admit it; the back story is that I have a long-standing aversion to Pot Luck (unless I am asked to BRING something TO one. In that case I love rising to the occasion and getting on my culinary mojo.) I, however, never wanted to HOLD a potluck, because it always seemed a bit, erm, cheesy to me. (I have no idea where I got THAT stupid idea!) So, I ran the idea by some of my best, most foodie friends, who gamely said, 'THAT WOULD BE GREAT!'

I confess that I micro-managed the food a bit...I do not like macaroni salad...but I have to say, what they brought was SMASHING! The food surpassed my wildest expectations, and everyone really enjoyed it. Including ME. It was just the best brunch EVER.

We had an elegant post wedding brunch in my sweet and generous friend Danielle Lin's beautiful living room. It satisfied my craving for beauty and sophistication. White tablecloths, crystal, china, flowers. It was a WOW! My friend Paula did the arrangements and the styling of the party (and much, much more...) and it was gorgeous.

Is this the point of my story? Not really. The thing that I REALLY learned was that asking my beloveds to contribute food to our wedding was the BEST way to come together as a community. It made our wedding into much more than the sum of its parts. So, I was able to let go of a rigidity that I had about "Pot Luck" and how a wedding should be run and see that coming together to share food and witness our union was the BEST way to do it. To quote the A Team: 'Don't you love it when a plan comes together?' My friend Rich observed that, 'This wedding was a gift to everyone who attended.' I had to agree. It certainly was a gift to my shiny-new husband and me. A precious, intimate moment of sharing and connection. Can you remember letting go of a rigidity and actually enjoying yourself?

Editor's note: Suzanne is a teacher and facilitator of The
Now Technique™ and has a website:
www.suzannemark.com
and a blog at
www.suzannemark.wordpress.com.

PREJUDICE AND SELF ESTEEM

After a delightful luncheon in the Atlanta loft of a member of a group I co-founded called Eclectic Ladies Network, we gathered around for the second part of the monthly event. Included in the invitation to each of these gatherings is a cleverly composed question meant to evoke personal experiences and lessons which we all share with one another. I will always remember that afternoon because the question was "Who was your mentor and what did you learn from your mentor?" The responses were as varied as the women in attendance—we are all ages; we come from diverse ethnic and cultural backgrounds. Twenty nine women paid homage to their most cherished teacher, mentor or life coach and shared the pearls of wisdom passed along to them. One memorable lesson that has remained with me and has enriched my life is the story shared by Tayyibah Taylor.

Tayyibah Taylor

She is the publisher and editor-in-chief of Azizah Magazine, a powerful publication that reaches well beyond the acknowledged audience of the contemporary Muslim American woman. While some articles are faith related, much of the material is food for thought for intelligent women everywhere. She was born in the Caribbean and moved to Toronto when she was seven. It was the first time she found herself not of the dominant culture and the first time she experienced racial prejudice. She related how she saw no images of people of color in the media, textbooks or magazines, except when imparting a negative image. Despite having noted professionals in her family and among family friends, she still internalized a sense of inferiority. Her father was a chemical engineer for Texaco Oil Company, and it was not unusual for Tayyibah to return home from school and sit at the dinner table among scientists, doctors, educators and lawyers from around the world.

One day while in high school, she experienced a painful incident of racism. When she relayed the various prejudicial experiences she was having, her parents shared a mighty lesson with her: "Never allow someone else to judge your value. Don't define yourself by how others see you. Look within and know that you are a spiritual being having a human experience. No one is better than you, and you are better than no one else." Their continued love and support have shaped the outstanding woman that she is today. She travels the world delivering speeches, meeting high level politicians, and visiting villages and people in third world countries—delivering a message for change, love and support.

I thank Tayyibah to this day for sharing that awesome story with us. It applies to us all regardless of the circumstances. Women are especially too quick to compare and judge ourselves by others' standards. The lesson learned: look at another being as a spiritual being on this earth walk. Look beyond color, gender, body shape, looks, and see others as human spirits. The body is the shell of the person; it is what lays within that makes each one special.

PREJUDICE TAKES MANY FORMS

Prejudice comes in many disguises. I learned that life lesson years ago when I was thirteen years old. Growing up in a middle class neighborhood in the Chicago area, we had neighbors and friends from many different backgrounds. That changed when my family realized the "dream" of moving to an upper class suburb of Chicago. Our home was larger than we could ever imagine, and our neighbors changed from salesmen and factory foremen to attorneys and architects. Neighborhood cars went from Buicks to Cadillacs. Lawns were manicured by landscapers instead of their owners and houses were cleaned by hired help instead of Moms or Dads. The problem was that while our circumstances had changed, our behaviors and way of life did not. To make matters worse, we are of Italian descent, and while we were tending to our own yard, were sometimes mistaken for the landscapers. We were the Beverly Hillbillies.

In short, we didn't fit in. Not because of issues like integrity or neighborliness, rather because of our lack of sophistication and social status. We cleaned our own home, mowed our own grass and were not charter members of any club or museum. A nanny did not watch our children – my mother did. As a result, with the exception of a few kind neighbors, we were shunned by most others. My brother dropped out of high school. My five year old sister was pushed down at school and shattered her elbow, requiring weeks of traction in the hospital, and I was taunted by my 7th grade algebra teacher. We lived there for one year, and returned to a more middle class neighborhood where we fit in.

For the most part, I didn't understand what was happening until sometime after the ordeal had ended and I was older and able to put the pieces together. I never disliked any of my neighbors, but they disliked me. Through my life-lens, people were basically the same – yet through their life-lens, some people were better than others. Prejudice is painful – and the results can last a lifetime. Luckily, I was too young to fully understand it, and the experience was short, with no lasting effect – except the life lesson.

To this day, 43 years later, I have an admiration for "regular" people and approach the wealthy and powerful with caution. I have learned that prejudice takes many forms and does not limit itself to race or skin tone. It shows up in economics, religion, education, appearance and talent (or lack thereof) and it can infect rich and poor neighborhoods alike. I have been blessed to know people from many walks of life, including wealthy people who use their good fortune for others and "regular" people who look down on others, but this life lesson has taught me to seek a person's inner character before looking at their station in life.

Editor's note: the author of this story preferred to remain anonymous. That is his prerogative.

PROFOUND LESSON FROM SOUTH VIET NAM

Cathy Horvath

I was comfortably ensconced in a "spa" chair at my favorite salon getting my nails done one recent afternoon. I know most of the nail technicians by sight, but not by name. They are all from different villages in South Viet Nam and their names are difficult to pronounce, let alone remember. Some have taken on "American" names like Jane, Susan and Barbara.

As I sat there I watched one particular nail technician walk past me several times. She would answer the phone to take appointments, fold the hand towels from the dryer, and then just sit and read a magazine until the next client arrived. She seldom engaged in conversations with the other ladies. I couldn't help but think to myself what a sad expression she had on her face. She never smiled that afternoon or any other. I thought to myself, "She must be a very unhappy lady. Maybe her husband beats her. Maybe she has serious money problems. Maybe she's sick or has a seriously ill relative. Something very sad must be going on in her life. But I will never know." (Or will I?)

A few minutes after those thoughts whirled around in my head, I asked my nail technician, "Susan" if she would like to contribute to this book. I suggested perhaps she could relay the story of how she and her husband "Johnny" met. Her son is attending Culinary School and I asked if he would translate a Vietnamese recipe for me. I knew a little of their life story and I knew that she still cooks Vietnamese foods at home for her family.

"You could write about your escape from South Viet Nam during the war and your life in the encampment in the Philippines. You could write about how you and Johnny met there and married." I suggested.

"You should ask the others about leaving Viet Nam and what it was like during the war." she said. Her response opened a Pandora's Box of tales of escape, terror, slavery, beatings, near starvation and finally relocation to the United States of America. All the technicians shared their horror stories as well as their joy in coming to America and living in freedom.

Joanna left her family behind and spent seven long days and nights walking through the forest, hiding from North Vietnamese soldiers, and nearly starving until she met up with other refugees who sought safety from the war and the terror of the Communists. Thousands walked to Cambodia only to be sold into prostitution, to live in horrific conditions of poverty and for many – to die. The others told of thousands that fled to the ocean only to drown. They shared their stories of escape. Anything was better than staying in Viet Nam.

"Louise" shared how she eventually made her way to the U.S. She is married and has a family now, but she is adamant about not spoiling her kids. She is determined to make them appreciate what others take for granted and to earn money for the things they want. She does not take her freedom and new life for granted.

Now I know why the first technician's expression is so sad. Her horrible life experiences stay with her and are an integral part of her persona. As we engaged in conversation, difficult though it was at times to understand, she opened up about her history as if it were the first time someone other than her own countrymen wanted to know all about it. Joanna is a lovely lady, and I thank her for teaching me something I should already know: Talk with someone who seems to be hurting. Find out what I can do to help. Perhaps an ear is all that is needed. Never Judge! You Never Know!

PUERTO RICAN TURKEY

Judy Slack is a friend I met early on in my career in the relocation industry. She was always eager to share her knowledge and help with a project when approached. She remains the consummate real estate agent in the San Diego area. She writes:

Judy Slack

This recipe has become our "house special" for all parties at our home over the years! In 1976, our middle daughter was swimming on a competitive team in San Clemente – and we attended a "Team Barbeque" at one of the swimmer's home. The host, Dr. Luis Santaella, originally from Puerto Rico, served this awesome turkey, a recipe from his homeland – hence the given name, Puerto Rican Turkey.

We have cooked it so many times over the past 30 years – the only difference is the original recipe calls for baking it in the oven like a normal Thanksgiving Turkey. My husband Bill improvised – and we prefer the turkey cooked on the Weber Grille. This turkey has been the table food centerpiece at tailgating parties at the Hollywood Bowl, the San Diego Chargers games, UCLA games, and even went to the Rose Bowl game in 1999. It has graced the fanciest of Thanksgiving tables as well.

In short, whenever we are invited to a party where we all share in preparing the food, guess what we are asked to bring? If we invite folks to our home, they invariably ask if we are serving the turkey! Occasionally someone still assumes that we fly the turkey in from Puerto Rico! Not!

PUERTO RICAN TURKEY

INGREDIENTS AND PREPARATION

For each pound of washed, and patted dry turkey, make a mixture of the following: 1 clove garlic, 1/4 teaspoon ground black pepper, 1/2 teaspoon oregano, 1/2 teaspoon salt, 1 teaspoon olive oil and 1/2 teaspoon red wine vinegar. Rub the mixture all over the turkey, inside and out. Put the turkey in a trash bag and place in a cooler with ice for 24 hours.

The next day, roast as usual. We have modified the directions by roasting on the Weber Grill on indirect heat. This is fabulous – the coating seals in the moisture and the skin is to die for! Enjoy!

Be sure you multiply the number of pounds by the ingredients listed. i.e. a 14 # turkey would need 14 teaspoons of olive oil in the mixture.

RAY'S CHICKEN PAPRIKASH

This is my husband, Ray's, contribution to this book.

Ray Horvath

From as far back as I can remember, my parents would serve our family a Chicken Paprikash dinner accompanied by soft noodles. The recipe for "Paprikas Cairke" was handed down from their parents who immigrated to this country in the early 1900's from Hungary. I married a girl of Italian descent and we started our own family. My wife Cathy (author of this book) was a stay at home Mom. She did all the cooking and baking and loved introducing new recipes to me and our four children. One day I decided to give her a break and prepared this dish. I was a little apprehensive because it was different from the "American" or "Italian" dishes we usually ate. To my amazement they all loved the meal and asked for second helpings. I really started something because ever since then I have been requested to prepare "Dad's Special Dish" quite often. When our grandchildren came along, all six of the little "picky eaters" were introduced to the same meal.

Their response was the same: 'Grandpa, this is really good!' It seems that for everyone's birthday they specifically request Chicken Paprikash. I find that quite amazing. You would think they'd want tacos or pizza or hamburgers.

We got a call one day from our grandson, J.J., who was away attending college in Illinois. He asked for the recipe so he could make it for his roommates and college buddies. He has even taught his mother, our former daughter-in-law, how to make it. I guess I'll always be remembered for my recipe, and the best part of all is that it has now been handed down to another generation. Isn't that wonderful?

RAY'S
CHICKEN
PAPRIKASH
RECIPE
ON THE
NEXT PAGE

HUNGARIAN
CHICKEN
PAPRIKASH

INGREDIENTS

1 - 3 lb chicken disjointed or all chicken breasts

1 large onion finely chopped

3 tablespoons of cooking oil

1 1/2 tablespoons of paprika

1 teaspoon salt

1 cup (8 oz.) sour cream

INGREDIENTS FOR SOFT NOODLES

3 cups of sifted white flour

1 teaspoon of salt

4 eggs

1/2 cup of water

PREPARATION FOR CHICKEN

Wash the chicken well, drain and pat dry. Then brown the onions in the oil until clear. Add the paprika, stir and then add the chicken. Sprinkle the chicken with salt. Simmer the chicken slowly for about an hour or until tender, turning the chicken occasionally.

PREPARATION FOR SOFT NOODLES

Mix all ingredients together and stir until smooth and velvety. Drop by 1/4 to 1/2 teaspoon into a deep pot of boiling water salted with a teaspoon of salt.

Cook for about 10 minutes or until they all rise to the top. Drain and then add to the chicken. Gently stir the chicken and the noodles, then fold in the sour cream. Just heat through—don't overcook the sour cream—and serve.

REED'S CHOKE CHERRY JELLY

Connie Siewert, a dear friend and author of *"A Skeptic's Guide to the Adventures of Life,"* has sweet memories (no pun intended) of her Dad preparing this recipe. A native of Grand Forks, North Dakota, Connie recalls anticipating this annual tradition in mid August or early September when the clumps of dark purple or almost black cherries were readily available in the surrounding countryside. They grow either in large bushes or small trees. It's interesting to note that they were a main staple of the Native American diet. I had heard Connie refer to

Connie Siewert

this recipe more than once and finally asked her to share it.

"My dad always made Choke Cherry Jelly as his goodwill currency and ceremoniously delivered his little homemade jars of jelly as if he had just bestowed a gift from Fort Knox. We didn't have a choke cherry (not berry) bush at our house. Dad had to cajole other people that had bushes to let him pick them with help he enlisted from neighborhood kids. In later years, he asked folks to simply give him part of the berries or even the juice they had collected themselves."

REED'S CHOKE CHERRY JELLY

INGREDIENTS

1 lb. choke cherries

water

4 1/2 cups sugar

1 box Sure Jell

PREPARATION

Wash, stem and boil the fruit in enough water just to cover for about 15 minutes or until soft. Crush and squeeze through clean cheesecloth. Measure 3 - 3 1/2 cups of juice. Place the juice and 1 box of Sure Jell in a large pot and bring to a rolling boil. Stir constantly so it doesn't burn. Add the sugar stirring well as the mixture comes to a rolling boil again. Boil one more minute. Skim the foam off the top and pour into sterilized jars.

Pour melted paraffin wax 1/8 inch thick over the top of the hot jelly. When cool, pour another 1/8 inch over the top. Prick the air bubbles. Store in a cool place.

Note: some recipes call for an addition of 1/2 cup lemon juice or 1 tablespoon butter. Try the recipe either way to determine the taste you like best.

REMEMBERING MY DAD

My father passed away a few years ago and after I left his funeral, I thought to myself "Well that's that. He's gone now. Life will be a little more peaceful now." Yes, he was gone physically, but I am surprised at how often memories of him continue to flood my consciousness. I was certain that I wouldn't be haunted by the hurtful things he said and did to me because he wasn't around anymore to talk to or visit. I was wrong. In spirit, he is very much alive.

Cathy Horvath

You see, he wasn't an easy man to love, and to the sad admission of family members and others, he did not leave a legacy of love behind. Or did he? This point was made clear to me when I read a newspaper article on Father's Day written by the daughter of a man with very similar traits and personality to my dad's. Her experiences and issues with her father really hit home. The only emotion expressed by the writer and her father was anger. Neither one said I love you all through the years of their lives. She had to dig deep, but she soon realized that he showed his love in many non-verbal ways. The writer ended the article by thanking him for all the things she had taken for granted, but were in fact, acts of love. She honored him that day by letting him know how much she appreciated him and yes, loved him.

My sisters and I were never allowed to talk back to our parents. The first time I did so was when I was 63 and I finally responded to some nasty name-calling and accusations from my father. Prior to that day, I listened in silence as he would criticize and judge me. I was respectful, just as I had been taught. I would think to myself, "I haven't lived up to his expectations, therefore he doesn't love me. He never told me he loved me. My assumption must be true."

However, after reading that article and engaging in reflection, I have come to the conclusion that my father did love me—in his way. Working two jobs to put food on the table and clothes on our backs was an act of love. He even worked side jobs in between times. After I was married, he helped paint our new house, came to our rescue when our cars broke down, fixed things when we couldn't afford a repairman, and kept my four month old son alive when our baby was so sick he refused all foods and liquids. All Dad did was take my son in his arms, talk to him, pick up the bottle with Jell-O water and got our baby to drink for the first time in twenty four hours. When that same son, at age 12, was hit in the head with a baseball at school and was hospitalized, Dad and Mom drove immediately from North Central Arkansas to our home in the Chicago suburbs. Dad stayed with my son and helped him when we brought him home, still dizzy but okay. Dad always pitched in to help family members and friends with repairs, or assist when they were ill, albeit begrudgingly at times, but he helped nevertheless.

So here's the lesson I've learned: He did the best he could, given the circumstances of his childhood. He was demeaned and denigrated by parents and siblings alike. He didn't have a role model for good parenting skills. And actually, back then in the 40's and 50's, the same can be said for many folks of that generation. He had some traumatic experiences in his lifetime. He was controlling, hurtful, and emotionally abusive to my mom and the rest of us. He could have mended his ways because he was aware of the pain he caused and seemed to gloat in it. The older he got, the worse he got. Yet none of us stood up to him and made him accountable for his actions.

Enough about that and back to the lesson. I remember part of Emperor Julius Caesar's speech on the steps of the Roman Forum to the Senate that went something like this: "The evil that men do lives after them; the good is oft interred with their bones." So here's my point: Whenever my mind reverts back to the painful memories of my Dad, I choose to replace them with memories of the good and kind things he did. That helps me a lot and I'm sure it helps him wherever he is. I haven't forgotten, but I forgive him. I am at peace now.

RETIREMENT LESSONS

Cathy Horvath

Have you been anticipating retiring in the near future or sooner? Do you have friends or family members who have retired? If the answer is Yes to these questions, you may want to sit down over a cup of coffee and have a heart to heart talk with whoever falls into that category or your significant other. It will be worth your time. A few years ago, I was brought in as a speaker for the Pre-Retirement Program sponsored by AARP that a major corporation in Chicago conducted for its employees who were in their mid forties. Once a week the Human Resource Dept. brought in a professional speaker such as a financial planner, an attorney, a psychologist, a physician, etc. As Vice President of a large real estate company, I covered the topic of housing alternatives and relocating to a new area. It was a wonderful program and I wish every employee in this country could participate in such a program while they are in the prime of their careers. There seems to be a plethora of material presented by the media these days to cover most of these topics, but I'd like to share some personal experiences and lessons that I learned from family and friends.

First of all, many folks talk about moving to a warmer climate or a less expensive part of the country the day after they retire. It sounds good but there is a lot more to it that, unfortunately, is not often taken into consideration.

Take my parents, for example. They were lifetime residents of Chicago. My dad took an early retirement from the Chicago Fire Dept. and they moved to Mountain Home, Arkansas, a small town in the Ozark Mountains twenty four miles south of the Missouri border. It was a ten hour trip by car from Chicago where we lived, so our family visits were limited to holidays and summer vacations. It was a big adjustment for my folks to start over in a new place where they didn't know anyone, much less to lose the frequent "pop in" visits from family and friends they were used to back home. It took a while for them to get re-established, but the most difficult part was not seeing their old friends and not being a part of their grandchildren's lives. My mom used to say that, although she made several new friends and the neighbors were very nice, it just wasn't the same. The friends back home shared a lifetime of experiences together and their bonds became stronger as each year passed. On a more serious note, a pattern began to evolve in their town whereby folks enjoyed their early retirement years, but as illnesses became more serious and they could no longer care for their spouses or themselves, the eventual move back home to be near the kids was the ultimate relocation.

Another point to consider: Unless you've managed to save a substantial amount, money will be tight and you will think twice about buying something for yourself or the grandkids. Cutbacks will follow for many of the activities you used to take for granted. Have you checked out the cost of an evening at the movies that includes a Coke and a box of popcorn? We now subscribe to Netflix. Have you experienced the cost of a cup of coffee and a muffin at a local café? I bake. Several gals I knew who used to enjoy the treat of getting their hair done frequently now cut their own hair and dye their hair from a box. Dinner for two has become a pricey treat even at the most reasonable restaurant chains. We cook at home and save leftovers. Gas prices make the trips to visit friends and family less frequent. You don't trade in your car as often as you used to despite rebates and low interest rates—it's still money out of pocket.

How much fishing and hunting can you do day after day? How much golf can you play week after week? While you're gone what will your wife do? I know personally of a friend that retired to Florida from the North. Leaving the cold and snow behind was a dream come true. However, they were a one car couple which meant the wife remained home alone for days while hubby played golf and had a few beers with the guys. She was so lonely and depressed; she almost had a nervous breakdown. Solution: buy another car which meant

more insurance, more gas, and more repairs bills. More money spent that they didn't anticipate. But the wife is a happy camper now.

When the wife has a great career going that she has worked hard for and enjoys, how do you decide when to retire? If the man retires and the wife continues working, the dynamics of the household change. Who pays the bills, who shops for groceries, who goes to the cleaners, who cooks? "Well, you're home most of the day, why don't you do it?" Oh, oh, you need to talk.

Then there's the big emotional adjustment which I touch on in another page in this book. If you identify yourself by who you were or what you did in your career, it's another adjustment. I catch myself so often referring to my previous career. "When I was a _____ I used to, or I did_____" Now you have to create another you. It's really a big help to start a hobby or create an interest while you're still in pre-retirement mode. Doing so affords you the opportunity to create a new circle of friendships outside the workplace.

There's a lot of good that comes with retirement. Time to do the things you've set aside all these years. Time to be with family. Time to learn new skills. Take a class. Join a club. You get the picture. However, retirement goes a lot smoother if you give plenty of thought to some of the points I've made.

Rosanna Magnani

RISOTTO CON ZUCCHINI E PESTO

Risotto with Zucchini and Pesto

INGREDIENTS

4 cups vegetable broth
(or water)

3 small zucchini,
about 3/4 lb. altogether

2 garlic cloves, crushed

2 tablespoons finely chopped
parsley

1 1/2 cups raw rice

2 tablespoons butter

3 tablespoons pesto sauce

1/2 cup freshly grated
Parmesan cheese

PREPARATION

Bring the broth to a boil and keep just below a simmer. Trim the ends of the zucchini and cut into thin slices. Heat the olive oil in a large saucepan and cook garlic and parsley for 1 minute. Add the zucchini slices and cook over moderately high heat until golden on both sides. Add the rice and cook 1 minute so each grain is coated with oil. Reduce heat to medium or low depending on the stove. Add a ladleful of broth. Repeat until the rice is tender but still firm and all the liquid is evaporated.

Stir in the butter and pesto sauce. Serve at once with grated cheese on the side.

Serves 4

ROBYN'S MASHED POTATO CASSEROLE

This is my daughter's recipe that she received over twenty years ago from a friend of her husband's family. It is such fun to share recipes with your grown children. I used to be the Horvath Family Kitchen Diva. Now I share that status with my daughters and it is delightful!

Robyn Huber

ROBYN'S
MASHED
POTATO
CASSEROLE

INGREDIENTS

8-10 medium potatoes

1 8 oz. package cream cheese, softened

1 cup sour cream

garlic salt

chives

butter

paprika

1 8 oz. pkg. cheddar cheese, shredded

PREPARATION

Peel potatoes; cut into quarters and add to pot of water just a little more than to cover. Bring to a boil. Cook until tender; drain and mash. Beat cream cheese and sour cream at medium speed until well blended. Gradually add hot potatoes, beating constantly until light and fluffy. Season to taste with garlic salt; add chives. Spoon potatoes into a 2 qt. greased casserole. Brush top with butter and sprinkle with paprika. Top with cheese the last 10 minutes of baking. Bake at 350 degrees for 30 minutes. Serves 6-8 people.

(I also add some cheese to the potato mixture.) If you use instant potatoes, follow the instructions for eight servings and add approximately 1/2 cup additional potato buds to thicken if the results are too soupy.

ROSANNA'S RISOTTO WITH MUSHROOMS

My maternal Grandparents were close friends with Tarsilla and Alfredo Barsotti—all from the "old country"—Italy. They have all passed on now, but I asked their son to share some recipes for this book. To my surprise, he called upon his cousin Rosanna who lives in the coastal town of Viareggio (Tuscany) Italy to send him one or more of her favorites. Rosanna is the beautiful mother of two handsome men and a beautiful daughter. She is a young grandmother to five. Having a typical Italian family, Rosanna is called upon to cook for as many as twelve people most evenings, and over the years has developed an outstanding list of typical Tuscan dinners. Many of her recipes reflect the coastal town of Viareggio noted for its seafood. Others are typical of the nearby Apuan Alps and of the Province of Lucca.

Rosanna Magnani

RISOTTO CON FUNGHI ALLA VIARREGINA
Risotto with Mushrooms

INGREDIENTS

2 cups rice

3/4 cup dried porcini mushrooms

1 medium red onion

3 tablespoons extra virgin olive oil

3 tablespoons whipping cream

2 1/4 tablespoons salt

1/3 teaspoon peperoncino (Italian pepper also known as chili pepper, paprika, or Spanish pepper)

Parmesan cheese to taste*

PREPARATION

Place dried mushrooms into a bowl with 2 cups of warm water and let soak for 30 minutes. Add olive oil to a large frying pan and heat to medium high. Dice the onion and place into frying pan and sauté until slightly golden. (Do not over cook.) Remove the soaked mushrooms from the bowl (do not discard the water) and cut into small pieces. Stir the mushrooms in with the sautéed onions and allow to cook for a few minutes to blend the flavor. Filter the water of the soaked mushrooms and then add slowly to the frying mixture. Add 1/2 teaspoon salt and a dash of peperoncino*.

In a separate large pan add rice to 2 quarts of salted (2 tablespoons) water and bring to a boil. After 15 minutes, drain the excess water from the rice. Add the rice to the pan of onions and mushrooms, stirring while adding. Add the whipping cream and grated Parmesan cheese.

Continue to stir and cook about 1-2 minutes. Risotto is ready to serve.** BUON APPETITO!!!! It is recommended that a good Chianti wine be served with the meal.

* May be adjusted to taste.   ** May be adjusted to taste (al dente, or cooked through).

ROSEMARY'S EGG STRADA

Shortly after moving into our new home in Hinsdale, IL. I was asked to participate in a brunch potluck. Since I had never attended a brunch I was at a loss to know what to bring. My neighbor Rosemary offered the recipe that follows. Rosemary was a physician and a warm, lovely lady. I never met a female doctor before, let alone one that was a loving, caring mother, dutiful daughter, and wife. She never missed a ball game for each of her three sons, and took great care of her aging mother who ultimately came to live with them. She was a remarkable woman. I really liked her and respected her. She was very down to earth and she, too, taught me many lessons. She was not about affluence or image; she was all about God and family. I've had this recipe for over 30 years; I like the fact that you can make it the night before.

Cathy Horvath

ROSEMARY'S
EGG
STRADA

INGREDIENTS

2 lbs. bulk pork sausage

10 eggs

3 cups milk

1 1/2 teaspoons dry mustard

1 teaspoon salt

6 slices day old bread cubed

1 1/2 cups grated or shredded cheddar cheese

PREPARATION

Brown sausage, drain and cool. Mix remaining ingredients and add to sausage. Pour into 13x9 greased pan. Cover and refrigerate overnight. Bake at 350 degrees 1 hour until solid. Uncover the last 5-10 minutes.

SENATOR RUSSELL'S SWEET POTATOES

(Senator Russell was a very well known, long time Georgia senator when I was growing up.)

Jerry Connor

As a young wife, having the whole family over for the holidays was quite a challenge. In the beginning, we went to my grandmother's or my in-laws' home. Over time, each member of the family learned there were certain dishes that the family grew to expect and we had best not show up without it. Of course there were the dishes that I, who fancied myself as a budding gourmet cook, would try from time to time. To my disappointment, the family didn't always appreciate my efforts and there was the occasional wisecrack like, "Where's the lavender stuff this year?"

My mother and I have always been the only family members to really like sweet potatoes, baked with a little butter. Nobody else would touch a potato dish that wasn't mashed white potatoes. We always had that dish available. However, I didn't feel like Thanksgiving was Thanksgiving without sweet potato soufflé of some sort. To my amazement and delight, the family chose this as my dish. The recipe I settled upon follows.

SENATOR RUSSELL'S SWEET POTATOES

INGREDIENTS

3 cups cooked, mashed sweet potatoes

1 cup sugar   3 eggs

1 tablespoon vanilla   1/2 cups butter, melted

TOPPING

1 cup light brown sugar, packed

1/3 cup flour

1 cup chopped pecans

1/3 cup butter, melted

PREPARATION

Combine potatoes, sugar, eggs, vanilla and butter. Beat with electric mixer for 2 minutes and pour into a buttered casserole.

Topping: Mix ingredients with fork and sprinkle on top of potatoes. Bake in a 350 degree oven for about 30 minutes. May be prepared in advance. (I always baked the potatoes in the oven first. I went a little heavy on the vanilla. I also learned to cut back a little on the sugar and the butter.)

Makes 4 servings

Rosanna Magnani

SFORMATO DI FAGIOLINI

INGREDIENTS

2 lbs string beans

3-4 eggs

grated Parmesan cheese
(to taste)

dash salt

2 tablespoons extra virgin
olive oil

2 tablespoons bread crumbs

beshamilla (see recipe below)

BESHAMILLA *(Béchamel Sauce)*

1 quart milk

1 teaspoon grated nutmeg

2-3 tablespoons flour

4 ounces butter

PREPARATION

In a large pot add milk, flour, nutmeg, and melted butter. Stir at medium heat until a cream is formed.

In a large pot add 2-3 quarts of water to which a tablespoon of salt has been added. Add string beans and cook at medium high heat for about 40-45 minutes. Drain water. Remove from pot and allow string beans to cool. Chop string beans into small pieces using "mezza luna" or chopping knife on wooden block. Place chopped string beans in a large cooking dish.

In a separate bowl, add eggs and beat while adding a dash of salt, and olive oil. Pour this onto string beans and stir lightly to get evenly coated. Pour the beshamilla onto the string beans and stir lightly to ensure they are evenly coated with the beshamilla. Sprinkle the breadcrumbs and Parmesan cheese evenly over surface. Place dish into preheated oven (350 degrees F) and cook for about 30 minutes. The resulting dish should not be too dry or soggy when fully cooked. Remove from oven and serve.

SHIFT YOUR BELIEFS – SHIFT YOUR LIFE!

I met Barbe Joye when I was an associate in the division she headed for a major relocation management company. She was then and still is, highly regarded in the industry. She advanced in her career by hard work, integrity, and sincere commitment to her clients and employer. We both left that company and went on to different roles in the industry. We were cut of the same cloth in many respects, and in our own fields of endeavor came to be highly visible and respected. Her contribution to this book really took me by surprise. Barbe Joye, of all people, brought to task?! She is the guru from whom all others in the relocation industry learn. Everywhere she goes she willingly teaches and shares her vast knowledge and experience. But I know now what she is sharing in her story. Sometimes the Universe has to hit us over the head before we open our hearts and listen to Divine Guidance. When it's time for a change, change will happen. Her story, in many ways, is similar to mine:

Barbara Joye

"This is a lesson that I am currently living and that is more than profound for me and the folks I share it with. It has taken me many years and many challenging moments to fully understand that my time in corporate America is coming to an end and my next life adventure is upon me. I am in the midst of making a life change—leaving corporate America and moving into my next life adventure—one of jewelry design, writing as book, and life coaching. The life lesson is to take the high road when one passes through transition.

A few years ago, on a bleak day in February, I had a meeting which I have come to term "the Ground Hog Day Massacre."

I received a phone call from the President of my division along with a person I purportedly reported to and asked to fly from Denver to Boston for a meeting. The meeting took about an hour and the long and the short of it was that I was brought to task for not being a team member and not respecting my "boss." The first accusation took me totally by surprise and the second brought with it some real pointed dialog regarding respect and positional power. At the end of a very emotional meeting, I went back to my room at the hotel (I had to fly in the evening before) and determined on the elevator ride to my room that I had to leave the company. I was angry, I was hurt, my ego was deeply wounded and I could not wait to get on the plane and begin my plan of departure. I decided, after much reflection and meditation, that I would leave on my terms. And that I would determine, with the help of my spirit guides and advisors, what next.

Instead of leaving a job, I decided to focus on going toward a new horizon. And I am.

It took 18 months – much gnashing of teeth and many hours of meditation to finally come to the realization that the two individuals at that meeting in February (the Groundhog Day Massacre) were angels in disguise. I am finally in alignment with my soul's need for a new venue and adventure. I have left the company taking the high road – thanking all involved for their role – and finding no fault in the process. The outcome is that the transition is easier than I expected. I am being honored by the company with an award trip to St. Maarten. I am working as a consultant for two months to ensure smooth transition (this aids in some of the financial concerns) and in general I am having a delightful time with this transition.

The lessons of recognizing angels and thanking all of the events of our lives – the good, bad, and ugly ones – as having value and purpose truly results in gifts from the Universe.

I would recommend anyone making a transition – either by what appears to be their own decision or the decision of others – to appreciate the fact that the transition may well be the soul's need (not the Ego's want) and to honor it and all who assist.

Recently, I have made a shift in my own identity, taking the pen name Barbara Joye. I have published my own book, 'The Light Won: A Tutorial in Co-Creation.' This launch has created opportunities to be on numerous radio and podcast interview shows. I am being featured in articles in several magazines, one of which is an upcoming article in Pure Inspiration, and have been booked for several speaking engagements around the Denver metro area.

Yes, Barbe J. Ratcliffe has become Barbara Joye with the launch of the book 'The Light Won' and with the renewal of my Re-Invention Life Coaching business and appearances as The Shift Guru. The Light Won supports each and every individual to Shift Their Beliefs so they may create the life they desire. They can order my book and utilize my service offerings by going to www.theshiftguru.com and clicking on the Products tab at the top. Anyone ordering the book will receive a 20% OFF coupon for a Re-Invention Life Coaching session. These sessions can be done over the phone – they are available to everyone. Shift Your Beliefs – Shift Your Life!"

Barbe J Ratcliffe/Barbara Joye, The Shift Guru
303-880-5950
www.theshiftguru.com
www.TheCreatingFormula.com

SPAGHETTI LASAGNA

My friend Arlene Vanderbilt writes: "This casserole can be frozen and baked later. However, thaw in the refrigerator overnight and let it come to room temperature before baking. I always double this recipe since it makes great leftovers. When my three girls were in the primary grades, a former college roommate, who was living in California, came to visit. She said this recipe made a big hit at a recent bridal shower there and that my girls would love it. They did and now their children request I make it whenever we have a celebration. Enjoy!"

Arlene Vanderbilt

SPAGHETTI LASAGNA

INGREDIENTS

8 oz. uncooked spaghetti or other thin pasta

1 clove garlic, finely chopped

1 tablespoon butter

2 lbs. lean ground beef (ground round is good)

1 teaspoon sugar, salt and pepper

2 cans (8 oz. each) tomato sauce

1 can (6 oz.) tomato paste

1 small pkg. (3oz.) cream cheese, softened (use more if you wish)

1 cup (8 oz.) sour cream (I add more here too.)

6 green onions, chopped

1/4 cup (2 oz.) grated Parmesan cheese

PREPARATION

Preheat oven to 350 degrees. Boil spaghetti in large saucepan of salted boiling water until almost tender. Drain and set aside.

Heat butter in large skillet over medium heat. Add garlic; cook and stir 1 minute. Add ground beef and sugar; season with salt and pepper. Cook and stir until beef is no longer pink; drain fat. Add tomato sauce and tomato paste; simmer 20 minutes, stirring occasionally.

Meanwhile blend cream cheese and sour cream in medium bowl until smooth. Add green onions and mix well.

Spread a little meat sauce in 2 quart casserole to prevent noodles from sticking. Layer half of spaghetti, half of sour cream mixture and half of meat mixture. Repeat layer. Sprinkle on Parmesan cheese. Bake 45 minutes or until heated through.

Rosanna Magnani

SPIEDINI RUSTICI
Rustic Skewers serves 4

INGREDIENTS

2 pork chops

1 chicken breast

1/4 pound sirloin beef

1/4 pound Italian sausage

1 tablespoon extra virgin olive oil

2 green, red, or yellow peppers

1 1/2 cups white wine

8 skewers

1/2 chicken bouillon cube (or 1/2 cup chicken broth)

1 clove garlic

2 stems of rosemary

1 pkg. risotto

2 packages fresh cleaned Italian salad

Salt & pepper (Italians use red pepper instead of black) as desired to taste

Extra virgin olive oil and balsamic vinegar and salt to taste for salad

PREPARATION

Cut meat and peppers into 1-inch cubes and sausage into quarters. Place onto skewers alternating selections of meat then peppers. Place filled skewers into an adequately sized rectangular pan. Spread olive oil over meat and add salt and pepper. Dice clove of garlic and add to pan along with rosemary. Place pan on stove and set heat on medium-high to brown meat. Rotate skewers to ensure even browning of meat. When meat is browned, lower heat to medium. Add white wine and bouillon cube (or chicken broth) and cook slowly for 30 to 40 minutes. For first 15 minutes cover pan with lid or aluminium foil to allow enhanced wine flavoring.

Risotto cooking instructions (follow instructions on package) or in a separate 4 quart pot, add twice the amount of water as rice and bring to boil. Add rice and reduce heat to simmer. Allow rice to cook for about 20 minutes or when ready. This should be timed so that risotto is ready when meat is cooked.

Salad: In a separate bowl add the salad and season with extra virgin olive oil and balsamic vinegar to taste. Add salt and pepper to taste as well.

Serving: On each plate place 2 skewers and a large spoonful of risotto on the side. Add a spoonfull of sauce from the cooked meat pan onto the risotto and meat. Place a cluster of fresh salad on the side of each plate as well. A thin slice of fresh garlic can be added over the salad if desired.

STUFFED PRUNES, APRICOTS, and DATES

Jerry Connor

Born in 1943, I was still young during the Korean War. My mother, sister and I lived with my grandparents. "Bigmama," as we called her, was an especially giving person and she organized a "Cans for Korea" campaign. In those days, coffee came in tin cans. To open the can, there was a "key" you hooked onto the tab, and then twisted around until the lid came off. (You had to be careful as it was easy to cut yourself!) We collected the larger of those cans, and then stuffed them with small items the soldiers could use. We left enough room in the cans to include food that would not spoil easily; harder, drier cookies (mandel bread), hard candies and stuffed prunes, apricots and dates. Then we would tape them up tightly and mail them off. We also used to make these around the holidays. It was a special treat to get something that was not sold in stores and was so different. I have fond memories of making and eating these sweets.

STUFFED PRUNES, APRICOTS and DATES

INGREDIENTS AND PREPARATION

Take the pits out of all the fruits. Slice the fruits in half while leaving the two halves still attached so you can fold them over the stuffing. (The apricots usually came already pitted and in two separate halves.)

Using a metal colander, spread the fruit, inside part down, lining the colander. Steam until soft, but not too soft. While the fruit is steaming, cut large marshmallows in half and have pecan halves and a bowl of sugar available. Also, cut 3"x 3" wax paper squares.

When the fruit is ready, stuff each fruit with 1/2 a marshmallow and one pecan half. Close the fruit "sandwich" and roll in sugar, coating all sides. Now, place in the middle of a piece of waxed paper. (The size of the paper will depend upon the size of the chosen fruits.) Roll the paper around the stuffed fruit and twist the ends, the way saltwater taffy is wrapped. These will need to sit a few days for the sugar to liquefy, yielding a wonderful blending of flavors. (My favorite was always the prunes!)

SWEET PICKLED WATERMELON

Shortly after moving to the Atlanta area, I met Mariette Edwards. She is a spunky, petite, dynamic woman whose appearance belies her intelligence, skills and professionalism. A native of New York who spent twenty years in human resource management, she is now captain of her own ship helping high achieving executives and professionals take their business or career to the next level. She writes:

Mariette Edwards

"For all the years I lived in New York with my mother and grandmother, I have no recollection of my grandmother actually cooking anything except for wonderful Sunday dinners. So I was amazed and quite surprised to discover two recipe contributions from her in the Victory Memorial Hospital Cook Book published in Brooklyn, NY in 1920 by The Women's Auxiliary. The recipes give the reader an insider's glimpse into the housewife's life in the twenties. If you are curious, an online search will take you to a page where you can download the book for free. By the way, the recipe below calls for '4 tablespoons of cinnamon sticks.' Given that she was not much of a cook herself, perhaps my grandmother thought that was an accurate way to measure!"

SWEET PICKLED
WATERMELON

INGREDIENTS

4 cups vinegar

8 pounds sugar

4 tablespoons whole cloves

4 tablespoons cinnamon sticks

Watermelon

PREPARATION

Cut skin from watermelon. Cut rind into small pieces about 2 inches square. Cover with water, and cook until tender.

Boil sugar and vinegar 10 minutes. Add spices tied in a bag, simmer until syrupy, about 2 hours.

Add melon and simmer 1 hour. Fill jars and seal.

TAKING THE STING OUT OF DIVORCE

My best friend Joan's divorce from her husband of thirty four years provided her with one of the biggest lessons in her life. Her story is not that unusual, given the high divorce rate in this country. But she has given me permission to share it, with the hope that the peaceful dissolution that came about would be of benefit to others.

Joan Kesman

Their marriage had been rocky for many years, but Joan wanted to wait until all four daughters were grown and out of the house. Her husband talked her out of her first request for the divorce. They tried therapy, but he didn't follow through on the advice he was given and quit. Their ongoing incompatibility made Joan even more determined to strike out on her own. They fought a lot throughout their marriage, and she feared the repercussions of her determination to divorce him this time. Usually there would be a big fight, lots of anger, and it would be horrible. She didn't want that. She figured there had to be a better way.

With the help of therapy and meditation, Joan got to a place where she had the strength to get through the whole process of separation and divorce. She meditated every day and prayed to be rid of the anger she felt towards her husband. She visualized an amicable dissolution. She regained the self confidence she lost all those thirty four years. Joan was in charge of Joan—no one else. No one else could tell her what to do or how to do it anymore. No one could bring her down with insults and nastiness.

The divorce discussions went smoothly. There had been a noticeable change in Joan, so the dynamics of the divorce changed. She and her husband talked things over, wrote down how the assets were to be divided, and sought the same attorney for a quick and simple marriage dissolution. It worked!

It is enjoyable to listen to my dear friend relay the good times her entire family has over gatherings for birthday celebrations, holidays, or just meeting for dinner. Yes, I said the entire family—former husband, children, sons-in-law, and grandchildren. Joan's efforts affected the whole family and they have all benefited.

TERESA'S GRILLED JERK CHICKEN

Teresa Howe is Vice President, Client Development, Southwest Region NRT,

Teresa Howe

Coldwell Banker Residential Brokerage, Inc. She and I have been friends for many years. We've cheered each other for our successes, shared suggestions for generating new business, and always supported each other when the going got a little tough. She is an outstanding business woman, mother, wife and friend. This is her recipe:

"This recipe has been a favorite of mine for years. It has evolved over the years. My fondest memory of it is on my daughter's first birthday. We had just moved to Orange County two weeks before she was born. After one year, our friends from LA came to the party as well as our new friends in our new community. I made this for everyone and a great time was had by all making new friends and celebrating my baby girl's first birthday. My baby is 11 years old now and I am still making this. I have passed this recipe on to many people. You know a recipe is good when people want a copy."

TERESA'S GRILLED JERK CHICKEN RECIPE ON THE NEXT PAGE

TERESA'S
GRILLED
JERK CHICKEN

INGREDIENTS

1 medium onion quartered

1 garlic clove

2 Serrano chilies quartered (or you may use 1 Scotch Bonnet chili)

1/3 cup low sodium soy sauce

1/4 cup red wine vinegar

2 tablespoons light brown sugar

1 tablespoon olive oil

1 teaspoon ground allspice

1/2 teaspoon thyme

1/2 teaspoon black pepper

1/4 teaspoon ground cloves

1/4 teaspoon cinnamon

1 teaspoon rosemary

Pinch of salt

4-6 boneless skinless chicken breasts

PREPARATION

Combine the onion, garlic and the chilies in the food processor. Pulse until coarsely chopped. Then add the soy sauce, vinegar, brown sugar, oil and all of the spices and process to a thick runny consistency. (Add more chilies if you want a bigger kick.)

Marinate chicken for 2-3 hours. Turn the meat over half way through marinating time. You may also baste the chicken during grilling with the marinade. Enjoy!

Serves 4-6

TERRIFIC TUNA BURGERS

As young mothers with little money or places to take our small children, my friend and I took turns having lunch at our homes. We would either pack up little brown bag lunches and send the kids off to the backyard to play and picnic, or we would fix something relatively simple but delicious that we could all enjoy. She "took the prize" with the following recipe that I have served often to my kids and grandkids. It's still a winner today and I often wonder if she ever realized how famous her tuna burgers have become in our family.

Cathy Horvath

TUNA
BURGERS

INGREDIENTS

1 6 oz. can tuna, drained

1/2 cup diced cheese (American, Velveeta or whatever you prefer)

1/4 cup sliced green or ripe olives

1/2 cup chopped celery

1 small onion chopped fine

1/4 cup mayonnaise

PREPARATION

Combine ingredients. Slice and butter 6 hamburger buns and fill generously. Wrap each bun in tin foil and bake 20 minutes at 350 degrees.

THE ANGELS' GUIDE TO ABUNDANCE

With no particular topic in mind to discuss with my Guardian Angels, I often ask "What words do you have for me today?" One particular day, I received this answer:

Cathy Horvath

"Expect great things and they shall come to pass. The lack of expectation for possibilities and outcomes hinders humans. They are conditioned to believe great things do not happen. 'I don't deserve good things. Having abundance is not the 'Godly' way I had better not expect good to come to me.'

Yet this is exactly what you should be thinking. Abundance and great things are your right as a spark of God. Being created in God's image means you have a spark of the Divine Creator within you. God cannot create without leaving a part of God's self in that creation. Think about this. Anything you create is a part of you. Your consciousness created it in your mind; then, you made it happen. So that something is an extension of you, of your thoughts. You are an extension of the Creator's mind. Therefore all that is good is your legacy. Know that within each one is the power to produce abundance, joy and all that you consider abundance in your mind. Abundance is not always wealth. Abundance includes joy, good health and peace. So it is the human decision what existence shall be enjoyed. God will assist in the manifestation of your intent but you must be a willing partner. Pray for the outpouring of good in your life—relationships, health—whatever it is you desire. Since you and the Creator are a team in the creation or manifestation of your desires then remember to talk to your Teammate who is God the Almighty. God will listen but God needs to hear from you first. Give thanks for your current abundance and then ask your Teammate for assistance with that which you desire. Gratitude goes a long way. Find the good things in your life and let Him know you appreciate and recognize what is positive. Remind yourself of this as you walk through your day. Remember you are not alone—you have a Teammate who stands ready to help. In love and light dear one, we leave you with this thought to share with others."

THE ANGELS SAY

The angels say that the time has come for each one to reconsider his/hers life's path. Where are you going? Where are your actions taking you? Are you fulfilled? Are you happy? Do you make others happy? Have you made a difference in the world, if only with one small gesture at a time? Why follow the same path and expect life to be kind and satisfying when you are not experiencing kindness and satisfaction currently? Why expect peace on earth when there is no peace within you?

Cathy Horvath

There is a major shakeup going on in the world. You can make the decision to join the leagues of those who have made a choice to change directions and change their lives. You don't have to join a monastery or ashram to do so. Holiness comes from within no matter where you are or who you are, if you are living a life of integrity.

Those who choose to change honor their bodies by being more diligent about the foods they eat; they are careful about the chemicals they put into their bodies. They honor the earth with sound judgments about materials they use and/or discard. They have slowed down to smell the roses and enjoy the gifts from Mother Earth. They choose quality of life over quantity of possessions. They honor the Christ within each person that they meet and acknowledge that each has a soul that reflects the Divine Creator.

Remember, dear ones, that your life is important to God. It is His gift to you after all. What you do with His gift is clearly your responsibility. That is why you have free will. But don't be fooled—you will ultimately have to justify your words and deeds. Why not fix those habits that don't bring you joy and contentment? Why not change what does not honor His gift and watch for the change that takes place in your life. What a surprise is in store for you—we promise!

THE APPLESAUCE SAGA

Cathy Horvath

Every September I looked forward to receiving a bushel of Cortland apples from Wisconsin. My husband's co-worker made a special trip to a farm every year, and brought back a truck load for everyone that placed an order. It was an annual routine at our house. I baked a big pan of apple slices, and then made several batches of applesauce to freeze for the months ahead. In those days I baked and cooked a lot. Being what today is called a "kitchen diva" I had a well appointed kitchen. The décor included beamed ceiling, dark pine cabinets, country printed wallpaper, and an ivory countertop which featured a set of amber glass apothecary jars that I used as canisters. They were placed next to the stove and oven for easy access to main ingredients. They contained flour, sugar, salt, coffee and tea. This particular September, the routine was no different, except for the experience I will never forget as long as I live.

I spent hours that memorable day peeling, coring and chopping enough apples to make a big batch of apple slices. The recipe fills a 10x15 baking pan, so it took a lot of ingredients. The apple slices turned out great. I was so proud of myself. It was worth the effort, I told myself. I was getting a little tired, but I decided to keep going and make a couple of pots of applesauce to freeze for the winter months. So I peeled, cored, and chopped several more pounds of the apples. I put them into two large Dutch ovens, and stirred them until they started to cook down. Then I added the sugar from my canister and cinnamon, and kept stirring for a while. When they cooked completely down, I tasted each pot to see if I needed to add more sugar or cinnamon before turning off the heat. Much to my horror, I realized I had added salt instead of sugar! I was getting so tired from standing on my feet for hours preparing these recipes that I mistook the salt canister for the sugar canister. The two batches were completely ruined of course. I can't describe how devastated I was. How could I have done something so stupid after all the hours I put in?! I threw the contents of both pots in the disposal. The kitchen was a mess with pots and pans, apple peelings, etc. I looked around and decided I had to escape rather than clean up. I was either going to throw something in the kitchen and have a good old meltdown or I was going to get out of the house. I got on my bike and rode through the neighborhood for a couple of hours until I calmed down. It was a good decision. I couldn't afford to replace anything I would break. When I returned home, I emptied the contents of the canisters to their original containers and gave the canisters away. There is a sweet ending to this story, however.

In my absence, my husband finished mowing the lawn and came in the kitchen to see how I was doing. Once he saw the mess and realized I had left abruptly, he knew something was wrong. He cleaned everything up and by the time I returned, my kitchen was back to normal. We ate the rest of the apples. I just didn't have the enthusiasm to try for another batch of applesauce. We bought our supply at the grocery store that winter.

This is a fun project to do with your children so long as you monitor the stove. They are amazed at the outcome and proud of their participation.

APPLESAUCE

INGREDIENTS

8 pounds cooking apples, peeled, cored and cut into large chunks (you can use Cortland, McIntosh, Golden Delicious, etc.)

1 - 2 cups water

3 - 4 cinnamon sticks cut into 4 inch pieces

3/4 - 1 1/4 cups sugar (NOT salt)

1 1/2 tablespoons ground cinnamon (adjust to taste)

PREPARATION

In a large pot combine apples, water, cinnamon sticks and sugar. Gradually add the sugar and taste until the sweetness is satisfactory. Gradually add the water until the consistency is what you desire. Depending on the moisture of the apples, more or less water will be required.

Bring to a boil and simmer for about a half hour, stirring occasionally and breaking up the pieces of apples. When the apples are tender and the mixture is the consistency of a chunky puree, you can add the ground cinnamon and adjust the sugar to taste.

Cook a few minutes longer until the ingredients are blended. You can stop and serve or freeze at this point or put the applesauce through a food mill to make a smoother sauce.

THE BIRTH OF LINDA'S SON

Linda is as former business associate whom I and many others at the company admired for

Linda

her class, her successful career, and her sweetness. She had so many qualities that made her stand out among her peers. I am so appreciative of her willingness to share her experience and surprised that she kept this locked up in her heart for so many years.

"In May 1975, I was 20 years old, married and had a 2 year old child. After three years, it was proving to be a mistake due to my immaturity in life and love. I awoke one morning unable to straighten my legs and to get myself out of bed. I struggled to get to my 2 yr. old toddler, then to the phone to call my husband who was at work. He came immediately and we rushed to the emergency room full of fear as to what was wrong with me. After waiting 2 1/2 hours in the ER, the pain was worsening and my fear level was climbing. The 2 yr. old was impatient. Fortunately my mother-in-law was a nurse in the office of Internal Medicine Doctors located across the street from the hospital. We managed to get over to the office and one of the internists saw me immediately. He touched my legs, running his fingers along the back of my calves and knees and said, 'You have blood clots in your superficial veins, they could break loose and go to your lungs or heart at any time.' With that I was strapped to a stretcher and rushed back to the hospital where I spent the next fifteen days strapped flat in bed, not able to sit or even turn over for fear of the clots dislodging.

At the end of what seemed like forever and a battery of tests, medications, etc. the team of ten plus doctors decided I could go home. The caveat was that I remain on blood thinners and came back every other day for a blood test so they could adjust dosages if needed.

On one of my visits back, one doctor asked when my last period was and I realized I was clearly late in my cycle. A pregnancy test was run and I was 8 weeks pregnant.

This was a huge problem given the fact that I was still not out of the woods with the clots, and I was still on medication to try and dissolve them. Blood thinning medication can prove fatal for a fetus or cause many other problems. The team of doctors strongly suggested performing an abortion immediately. But I was 20 years old, married and needed my husband's consent. My husband was a recent born again Fundamentalist but we had never discussed his views on abortion. All I knew at my 20 years of limited wisdom was that this deeply concerned the doctors and the combination of being pregnant with the blood clots were not good at all. The doctors set up a meeting with my husband and me.

I recall sitting in an office with at least 6 doctors, an internist, a gynecologist, an obstetrician and others of various specialties in medicine due to the complexity of my situation. I had been on birth control pills which were still relatively new on the market and they all finally concluded that my clots were caused by 'the pill'. Nonetheless, a huge decision was at stake and time was of the essence.

The doctors began explaining the severity of my condition and how easily the clots still could dislodge and go to my heart and or lungs and kill me. They concluded with their recommendation which was to abort the pregnancy as soon as possible and for me to continue on medication to dissolve the clots which still threatened my life. My husband listened and finally said, 'She has a life inside of her and this is in God's hands now, she will carry that life and God will do as he sees necessary.' All of the doctors had a look on their face as though they could not believe what they had just heard. One finally responded and said, 'I'm not sure that you fully understand. Your wife's life is in danger here, she could die if she attempts to carry this baby, there is also the risk that the fetus already has damage due to the medications she has been taking, and we don't think her legs are strong enough to support the additional weight of a baby.' My husband responded quickly and in an angry voice and said, *'I don't care, she will carry this baby.'*

The next seven months were the most miserable, the most depressing months of my life. I had to stay in bed all but six hours a day. When I did get out of bed, I had to wear very heavy support stockings to stimulate circulation in my legs. My marriage continued to deteriorate. I struggled with carrying the additional weight of the baby and trying to take care of a 2 1/2 yr old toddler; my husband provided no support or assistance. I just wanted to die.

My due date was February 2, 1976. As the date drew nearer, my depression deepened. I was concerned as to whether I would have a healthy child or one with a disability. I reached a point that I didn't even care if I lived, if I died, or even if the baby lived. Two days before my due date was a Saturday, and my husband decided he would go hunting for the day. He spent the entire day in the woods. There was no way to contact him if I went into labor. He left me at home with no car and a three year old. He returned late that evening.

I was awakened at 5:00 A.M. the next morning with a huge contraction. It was a Sunday and we always went to the 9:00 A.M. church service. My contractions were approximately 30-40 minutes apart. When I declined to attend church and explained that I was having contractions, my husband reminded me of the lengthy labor I had with our first child and suggested this time would be the same. He thought I had plenty of time before we needed to go to the hospital. He finally agreed to let me remain at home, but left the three year old with me. His instructions were to call his parents (they lived 35 minutes away) if I felt that I needed to go to the hospital before he returned. When he returned, my contractions were about 25 minutes apart. We went to the hospital when they were 20 minutes apart. He dropped me off at the hospital, saying he would take the three year old to his parents and come back. I delivered 3 1/2 hours later and he was not there. I was scared of what was going to happen with this delivery and yet here I was all alone. I thought back to the day and about the words that he said to the doctors, *'I don't care, she will carry this baby.'* I knew that my marriage to him was over, no matter what the outcome of this delivery. One doctor had so much compassion for me through the entire pregnancy and ordeal. He had five sons of his own and was performing my delivery. He said, 'Linda, it's another boy!' I asked about ten fingers and toes. He informed me that he was beautiful and appeared perfect! I was finally taken to my room to rest. When a nurse told me that my husband had arrived to see me, I told her I didn't want to see him and I only wanted to see my baby.

I separated from my husband a year after the baby was born. We divorced and both remarried. I carried hatred towards him for 31 years for the statement that he made, *'I don't care (if she dies), she will carry this baby.'*

On Feb. 1, 2007, my son's 31st birthday, I was making preparations for his April wedding. It was then that I suddenly had a revelation. I realized that, had my ex-husband for whom I harbored so much hatred all these years, not made the decision to have me carry that baby 32 years ago, I would not be planning my son's wedding. Nor would I have had the wonderful bond and joy that I have had for the last 31 years! Suddenly all of the hatred melted away in that moment and I finally forgave him. I realized that God truly did watch over me during that time and gave me the most special gift that anyone could ever have. My son is healthy and wonderful and one of the most incredible people that I know."

THE FEARS THAT GRIP US

Nancy Wallace, intuitive life coach, was the catalyst for my spiritual journey, my connection with my Guardian Angels. My life continues to be enriched by her guidance.

Nancy Wallace

Her gift goes back to her childhood when she could see things happen before they actually did. She communicated with her angels long before others published books about it or made their abilities known publicly. She even does pet readings. She has amazing accuracy and is very well known and respected, having hosted a local cable TV show and radio show while living in a suburb of Chicago. She currently resides in Los Lunas, New Mexico.

I asked Nancy to share the most common thread that prevailed through thirty years of intuitive readings for people that have sought her guidance. She quickly and without hesitation answered: "Fear." I really didn't understand what she meant until she explained further: "Think about it—fear of failing (what if?), fear of not being loved (he/she won't love me if I....,) fear of not being worthy, fear of the unknown (if I do this, what will happen?,) fear of succeeding, fear of bodily harm (I might get hurt if I....) fear of death and dying and fear of lack of money."

"Fear holds us back from ever living our life purpose or fulfilling our dreams," she said. For example, she has seen clients sabotage their successes because of a belief of unworthiness.

They don't realize what they're doing until she gently guides them to this recognition. So I asked Nancy what she suggests her clients do to overcome this barrier to life's personal expression. "There are many ways a person can get past their fears. First you have to recognize that there is a fear. That fear is the block. Then it is important to know what made that fear consume you. When that has become clear, you need a way to get beyond the fear," she offered.

"Positive affirmations are a good place to start" she continued. Most people really don't know how to be positive. We are frequently reminded to think positive, but we really are not told how to do it. To think positive you must change the negative thoughts and words to make them positive. For example: to overcome the fear of not having enough money... say, 'What am I going to do with all the money that I now have?' So by changing the words and thoughts and putting that out to the Universe, the Universe has no choice but to return it the way you put it out. It's the Law of Attraction. What you focus your thoughts and energy on with passion and belief will manifest in your life. There is another thing a person can do. I call it 'The Let Go Letter.' The reader can find it on my web site: www.nancyspsychicresources.com. It is a good tool to rid oneself of the fears and blocks that keep you from your inner peace, prosperity and self fulfillment."

Editor's note: I recall reading a passage a long time ago that said "If you fear, you don't trust; if you don't trust, you don't believe in God."

THE KATRINA CHRISTMAS TREE

Myra and Emile's home in the New Orleans area was hit by Hurricane Betsy in 1965. The water rose to 5 feet in their house, so they had to gut it and start over. It was a tough experience for a couple in

their 30's, but they started over. Fortunately, they were able to salvage much of their possessions. Not this time. This time there was nothing to save. They lost their home and all their possessions during Hurricane Katrina.

They lived on the outskirts of New Orleans in St. Bernard Parish. Myra's sister lived with the couple and their daughter and two granddaughters lived four doors down on the same street. They all experienced the same tragedy—they lost all their possessions. At the urging of their son and brother, the night before the storm hit, they all packed up enough clothes for a two day stay and headed to his home in Dunwoody, Ga. Two days stretched into four months and longer for they never returned to New Orleans permanently. There was nothing to go back to—everything was demolished. "It looks like a war zone. Newscasts and newspaper accounts don't really show the extent of the devastation. You have to see it to believe it!" Myra told me as she relayed the wonderful story that follows.

Myra and Emile eventually moved to their new home in a small community south of Atlanta called Summer Grove. All they had at first was a mattress—no box spring, just a mattress. (They are in their 70's.) They had to start all over from scratch to fill the rooms and cupboards. Think about it—from furniture to pots and pans to spices and staples.

God smiled on them at last; the neighborhood they chose to live is filled with wonderful, caring people. All the neighbors liked to get together once in a while for social events. (barbeque, ice cream party, etc.) That particular year, the Halloween party turned out to be special. While munching away on hotdogs, chili, chips and dips, a neighbor asked Myra about how she and Emile survived the hurricane. Myra shared their horrifying experience. She related how she lost all of her possessions, but most importantly, the children's and grandchildren's photos, her wedding pictures, their Christmas tree and ornaments. The couple was married for fifty years when the storm hit. Myra had been a teacher in the reading lab for a Catholic school, and her tree was graced not only by the crocheted ornaments she had made, but the ornaments her pupils gave her through the years. How do you replace any of that she commented? "You can't," she said. End of conversation.

A few weeks later on a day in November, they noticed a scroll taped on their front door that read: *"Please be home on November 17th at 7 P.M. I understand you've been good and I've been talking to my elves. Love, Santa."* On the appointed evening around 7 P.M. the couple opened their front door to 30 Carolers, 15 on each side of the front sidewalk holding lighted candles in one hand and the other hand held behind their backs. They sang about three songs and Myra invited them in for coffee. "No, this isn't over yet; we've brought you Christmas tree ornaments." One at a time they deposited an ornament into a large basket—some brand new with the year on it, and some from their own personal collections. Myra and Emile thanked them for their kindness, and then the group escorted them to the house next door. "We're not done yet, so follow us" was their response. They promptly took the couple to the front of the next door neighbor's garage. When all had gathered, the door lifted and there in the corner was a beautiful tree lit with 1000 lights. The neighbors had all chipped in to buy the tree. Now, that tree will hold special memories for the couple. Okay, now it was time for hot chocolate and cookies and a wonderful celebration. It truly was a real celebration of the Christmas Spirit. Myra claims it's the best tree she's ever had.

Every person to whom I've relayed this story has been moved to tears. It is a lovely reminder that deep in our hearts, we are truly a caring society. Catastrophes like Katrina, disasters such as 9/11, fund raisers, and charities all bring out the best in human nature when men, women and children spring into action or dig deep into their pockets. I once heard a quote that is most appropriate to this story: "If you do not have the opportunity to do great things, you can do small things in a great way."

THE KUCHEN QUEEN

My friend, Peggy Graceffa, writes: "My recipe is from my mom, Margaret Mueller Barthel. In our family she was lovingly known as the 'Kuchen Queen.' To understand how proud our family is of her and her baking skills you need to know a little bit about her family history. You see my mom's mother, Leopoldina died in the flu epidemic of the early 1900's (1915 -1916). She left 5 children for her husband, Joseph, to raise on his own. My mom was the youngest, only three when she was left without a mother. My Grandpa did a wonderful job of raising his family…all married and had wonderful families of their own. Being the youngest, my mom had household chores fall to her when her older sisters married and moved away. Mom learned to bake basically on her own, through trial and error and some pointers from her dad. She could bake the best bread. Huge loaves that tasted wonderful, caramel rolls, cakes, cookies – you name it, she could bake it. She loved to try new recipes. She liked to write in her cookbooks about the recipes she made. When she died we found her cookbooks to be somewhat of a personal journal. She wrote dates and comments about the recipe or the occasion she was making the recipe for…holiday, birthday, and special dinner for friends, etc. But back to the 'Kuchen Queen'. Mom's favorite recipe was her Streusel Kuchen. We all loved it! She made Kuchen for every holiday or special family occasions. Many times she made it for no reason at all, just because we all loved Kuchen so much. As she had grandchildren, Mom would make small individual Kuchens, just for the babies. We have pictures of our kids eating the streusel off the top of the Kuchen. Even as babies they knew the best part! On Mom's 80th birthday, the whole family celebrated by taking her out to dinner and ordered a birthday cake with a huge crown that covered the top of the cake and the words 'Happy 80th Birthday to the Kuchen Queen.' We also got a crown from the party store for her to wear. She simply loved it!"

Peggy Graceffa

STREUSEL
KUCHEN
RECIPE
ON THE
NEXT PAGE

STREUSEL KUCHEN

INGREDIENTS

2 pkgs. (1/4 oz. each) active
dry yeast

1 cup warm milk
(110 – 115 degrees)

1/2 cup sugar

1 teaspoon salt

1/4 cup margarine

1/4 cup shortening (Crisco)

3 eggs, beaten

6 – 6 1/2 cups unbleached
flour

PREPARATION

Soften yeast in warm milk. Place sugar and salt in large mixing
bowl. Set aside. Heat and stir milk, margarine and shortening
until melted. (120 – 130 degrees) Add to mixing bowl along with
eggs and yeast mixture. Stir in 1 cup of flour at a time to form a
soft dough that can be kneaded. Knead in the remaining 5 1/2 to
6 cups of flour on a lightly floured board until smooth and elastic.
*(In her later years, Mom could not knead the dough as well and found
that she could use her KitchenAid mixer in place of kneading herself.)*
Place dough in a large greased bowl. Cover and let rise in a warm
place until doubled, about 1 hour. *(Mom used to heat the oven to
only 100 degrees, turn it OFF and put the dough in the oven to rise.
Be very careful not to get the oven too hot.)*

Punch dough down. Turn out onto a lightly floured surface.
Shape dough to cover bottom of a well greased pan. *(Mom used
square or round cake pans. Size doesn't really matter.)*

Shape the dough with your fist or hand in the pan to fit into the
corners or edges. Keep dough about 3/4 inch thick when finished.
Pour Karo or maple syrup on top of dough to make it just a little
sticky so the Streusel sticks better. Cover with Streusel (about 1/2
of this Streusel recipe on 1 Kuchen). You will get about 5 or 6
Kuchens from this recipe. Allow to rise in a warm place about an
hour. If she didn't have enough Streusel for all of the Kuchens,
she would make one with just cinnamon & sugar on top.

recipe continued on the next page

STREUSEL KUCHEN
continued

STREUSEL FOR KUCHEN

(Enough for 2 Kuchens) Triple this recipe. Divide among the Kuchens.

INGREDIENTS FOR STREUSEL

1 cup flour

1/2 cup sugar (white)

1 stick margarine

1 or 2 tablespoons cinnamon
(my mom used about 1 tablespoon
or more)

PREPARATION OF STREUSEL FOR KUCHEN

Combine with a pastry blender until crumbly. Then take your hands and squeeze it together to better blend the ingredients until you have crumbly "lumps" to put on the Kuchen. If you only use the pastry blender, it will not stick together in lumps on top of the Kuchen. *(We all looked for the piece with the big lumps….simply the best!)*

Bake at 350 – 375 degrees, depending on your oven for about 25 – 30 minutes. They should brown slightly and toothpick should come out clean.

P.S. Thanks Cathy for letting me share my recipe and story with you. It was just great reminiscing about my mom. And I have to tell you that for Easter this year, my daughter Liza and I made Kuchen for the first time. We said a lot of prayers to Mom to guide us and she must have heard us because the Kuchen turned out great! I did call my sister about 4 times through the process, but I know Mom was looking down and smiling at us.

THE ONLY CONSTANT IS CHANGE

As I watch the daily newscasts and witness the corruption in the corporate world both here and abroad; as trusted political hierarchies are exposed for their misdeeds; as weather conditions take the homes and lives of thousands of souls, I have turned to my Guardian Angels for comfort and advice. They have had a lot to say about all this, but I will share the latest communication with you in the hopes it brings you, too, some insight into your life.

Cathy Horvath

"These are indeed troublesome times for your country and for the world. Changes are all around you these days and the turmoil will continue to escalate for some years to come. Materialism is not the path to God. Your world has been obsessed with material possessions and collections. Collections are revered and displayed by those enjoying a wealthy status for others to envy. But the true person to envy is the one that is not possessed by their possessions. They enjoy them but are not obsessed. Prosperity and wealth is a gift from God. What is done with that prosperity and wealth, as we have said many times before, is the test.

Prosperity has been associated with financial wealth, status, and material possessions. In reality, those are fleeting and they are an illusion. What is true and everlasting prosperity is joy, inner peace, and love. The truth of our words is becoming more and more evident by the news as of late of those who have experienced untold wealth at the expense of others. Their wealth has dissipated and they are left with embarrassment, humiliation and near poverty.

That is not to say that being wealthy is a sin. It is the Creator's intention that all humankind enjoys the fruits of the earth, meaning abundance and good health. However, throughout the millennia, humankind has been influenced by greed, and has used violence to attain riches. Generations that followed have not learned from the mistakes of their forefathers and continue in their quest for riches through wars and violent acts. Have you learned nothing after all these years? Despite technological advances, are you really better off today than those in the societies of yesteryear? There are still those in power, religious and political, who vie for power; there are still those who covet another's riches and lie, steal, and connive to attain more and more riches despite the consequences to the trusting masses.

Enough is enough our dear ones. We have witnessed efforts to make changes and that is gratifying. When trouble rears its ugly head, where do you turn? To God, of course. What you don't realize is that He has always, always been there, not just at the moment of need. Get used to this idea. Talk to Him each day and listen in silence for His response. His response may not come immediately as you would expect. It may come with something that is said, something you read, a street sign, etc. But He will answer you in a way you will know. Fill your heart with a knowing that there is much more to life than what you can see, or touch. Prepare your hearts now for the changes."

THE TRAVELING COOK BOOK

This is sweet story from a lovely lady I have known for over thirty years. She is in her early 80's but you would never know it. She is sharp as a tack and just as beautiful inside and out.

"I received *The Betty Crocker Cook Book* as a wedding present from my sister when I married in 1948. My husband had served 4 years in the U.S. Air Force prior to our marriage and was recalled 3 weeks after our wedding day. A few days after his notification, we were on the train leaving Huntington, West Virginia and heading to Camp Pendleton in California. All the way out there, he kept saying 'the Air Force is going to have to retrain me.' (He was a pilot and had been away from flying for a couple of years.) Eleven months later I joined him in Guam.

A few days after my arrival, he invited 4 fellow officers to dinner. I had packed my cook book, a small aluminum frying pan and an aluminum coffee pot in one of the two suitcases I was allowed to bring with me. I made two pies in the frying pan using recipes from my cook book, baking one and then the other. Remember, in 1948, no one had heard of readymade pie dough so this took awhile. At that time chicken parts were not packaged so I had to cut up the chicken to fry. I cooked as many batches necessary to feed five hungry men. I boiled the potatoes in the coffee pot to make potato salad. Then I used the coffee pot to make iced tea. This took all day but it was worth it to see how much those guys enjoyed the meal. That experience taught me quite a lesson in that it is possible to do with less and make the most of it.

That cook book has traveled the world with me. 62 years later I still use it from time to time. It is stained and worn but I could never bring myself to get rid of it. God bless Betty Crocker."

THE WISDOM OF AGING

Cathy Horvath

*Remember friends as
you stand by.....*

*As you are now
so once was I....*

As I am now, so you will be...

*Think of this
and be kind to me.*

I have paraphrased a little poem that a Catholic Nun wrote on the blackboard when I was in high school. I can still remember that morning in Sister Virginette's Latin classroom at St. Willibrord High School on the South Side of Chicago. As the students took their seats, they watched her write these words on the blackboard. It was the week before Halloween. As Catholics, we celebrated the Eve of All Hallows on October 31 and then All Souls Day on November 1st. (Actually, the last sentence went: "think of this and pray for me.... from a poor soul.") I changed the wording to suit a different purpose, but I have come to use this little ditty often to remind people that aging is a process that can't be avoided. We seem to be a culture that has lost its reverence for the older generation. Take me for example: I don't have the body of a slender size 8 that I used to have, and I've lost a lot of the gorgeous hair on my head—over a third of it to be exact. My eyesight and memory aren't what they used to be

BUT—I possess something no thirty year old or even forty year old has yet: WISDOM.

I have to remind myself of that when I catch myself envying those sleek bodies prancing about on my television screen or featured in the magazines I read. Don't get me wrong; I am not unattractive, I am still complimented for my skin, and I'm not stupid. I dress as stylishly as I can, given my "adjusted" figure shape. I say "adjusted" because some of my parts have shifted from where they used to be. I still enjoy the opera, theatre, the symphony and museums. I love being around the younger generation. They are so intelligent and so techno-savvy. It's a marvelous world they live in with so many possibilities. I learn from them too. I like to be around younger people and soak up their energy and enthusiasm.

Wisdom can only come with age. My daughters approach me for guidance for everything from raising children to setting a gracious table, to their next career move. The same goes for my husband. Sons and daughters alike call Ray for handyman questions or help with a project. We are an integral part of our children's lives. We don't offer advice unless it is sought. But I think our family realizes that we have experienced a lot, learned a few lessons along the way (albeit sometimes the hard way), and may have something to contribute. As we grow older, we view things from a different perspective. We've learned what is important and what is not worth worrying or getting anxious about. There is calm or an inner peace that comes with age; a knowing that there is usually a way out or an answer to a problem. Sometimes we don't like to hear the answer, but there is one nevertheless. And when there seems to be no answer or a way out, we offer comfort, support and unconditional love.

I would hope that my words will inspire a renewed appreciation for what our senior citizens bring to our lives. A recognition that their eyes are mirrors to a lifetime of experiences, loves, travels, disappointments, and some wonderful stories to share.

TIRAMISU

My parents came to Canada late in life (my dad in his 50's and my mom 47.) I unexpectedly came along. They started a new life in a new country with a young son and a new baby. They started

Virginia Terkalas

with little money. They worked hard, bought a house, and sacrificed to give us a good life. My dad passed away February 10, 2001 at the age of 97 and my mom passed away December 14, 2010 at the age of 99. My children got to know and feel the love of their grandparents for many years. My parents are my inspiration for a long, happy life.

A special treat for us during holidays is a Tiramisu.

TIRAMISU

INGREDIENTS

1 tub mascarpone cheese (500 grams)

5 eggs separated

5 tablespoons sugar

Savoiardi cookies
(similar to lady fingers, available on the web or in specialty stores)

3 cups Espresso coffee

1 tablespoon of your favorite liquor (Amaretto, Kahlúa or Tia Maria)

Chocolate (powder or shaved)

PREPARATION

Separate eggs. Beat yolks and sugar. Add mascarpone cheese and beat. Beat egg whites till soft peaks form. Mix both together. Layer mixture in a flat bottom bowl. Mix coffee and liquor. Dip cookies in coffee mixture. Layer cookies in the bowl. Add 1/3 of the cream mixture. Repeat cookies and cream. Top with cocoa powder or shaved chocolate. Refrigerate overnight.

WHAT GOES AROUND....

Cathy Horvath

One afternoon in early September years ago, when the air was warm and the trees burst with brilliant oranges and golds, my new neighbor, Gloria, called to ask if I wanted to go for a stroll with our two toddlers. The older children had just started back to school. It was such a beautiful day and I thought the fresh air would do us both good, so I whipped through my housework, got the stroller out of the garage, and joined her. As women do, we chatted a lot about a variety of subjects as we walked. But one thing she said to me has remained in my memory ever since.

I was lamenting about how a few of my old friends seemed to be on the receiving side of my generosity and help, but never reciprocated by calling to see how I was, or doing something nice for me. I cited a few cases in point: I frequently brought a car trunk full of clothes and household items to one friend in particular. She was always appreciative and I was glad to help her out during several really tough years she and her husband were going through. My mom, aunt and mother-in-law would pool things for me to bring to her—she was in really dire straits. We always had a good time together during those visits, and I looked forward to having her company. What troubled me is that we never spoke on the phone unless I made the call to see how she was doing. I only heard about all her travails without being asked how things were going in my life. Some of those calls turned into rather expensive long distance bills when they moved out of state! That seemed to be a pattern that a few other friends experienced with her as well. We had wonderful times together as couples. But more often than not, Ray and I had to extend the invitations. Having these get togethers put a real strain on our food budget—things were tight for us too, but we did our best for those Saturday night parties and I made budget stretching meals for the rest of the week. My "friends" seemed to be takers and not givers. That hurt.

Don't get me wrong. I have always enjoyed helping out and rallying behind someone in need. I had been blessed with a supportive, generous family so it just seemed the natural thing to do. But once in a while I would have been delighted to receive a call to find out what was going on in my life and how the family was doing. I was a stay at home mom and new to the neighborhood, so I didn't get out much. A call from a friend would have brought some real sunshine into my life. Someone to talk to about my struggles would have been a real blessing at times—just to know I wasn't alone in what I was experiencing.

Back to the stroll with Gloria. I never forgot her response. "LESSON ONE: What goes around comes around, but not necessarily from the same person to whom you extended a kindness. It may not even come around in this lifetime, but there is a huge "bank account" in the Universe that remembers the good that one does. One day, someone out of the blue will extend a kindness quite unexpectedly. That's the payback. LESSON TWO: Don't bother doing something for someone if you expect a payback.

There is a blessing in giving without an expectation of receiving. Have you ever received an act of kindness from an unexpected source? That's payback—the Universe works like that. What goes around comes around, but not necessarily when you expect it and from whom you expect it." Gloria has since passed away after a long battle with the big C. She left behind a wonderful family and a friend who has never forgotten what I learned that day.

WHAT MY MOTHER NEVER TOLD ME.....

Cathy Horvath

No, it's not what you think; although she really didn't tell me all that much about sex and what to expect on my wedding night. I had to figure that out on my own. What she didn't tell me was what to expect when I entered my late fifties, into the sixties and beyond. I just entered the "beyond" stage a year ago. Having experienced multiple changes in my life, I realize that I need to prepare my daughters for the eventualities in theirs.

As I look in the mirror these days, I wonder who that woman is that is staring back at me. She doesn't look like the me that I have been used to seeing all these many years. Her body has morphed into a shape that requires clothing that is one to two sizes larger than she has ever worn in her life. Her face is full and her hair has thinned to 2/3 the amount that used to be there—on her head and other places that shall go unmentioned. It's hard not to get swept up into a deep depression. I know what the routine responses my loving family gives me. "Mom, you look great for your age." Or "Mom, this is life, this is how it goes. We love you just the way you are so don't worry about it."

Well, I'm not worried about it, I just didn't expect all this so soon. I don't really know what I expected and when I should expect all these changes. Some women look "old" at 50, others look great in their 60's, and I know several 70 year olds that you could never guess their age. So what's the rule? Wish I had some warning. In my mind I am still the "young me." This change requires a big mental and emotional adjustment and that takes time. I remember an old episode of The Golden Girls where Dorothy (played by Bea Arthur) just returned from a substitute teaching job one afternoon. Sitting at the kitchen table with the other gals as they so often did, she told of the wonderful conversations she had with the other young teachers in the teachers' lounge during breaks. She said something like "It was great to engage in stimulating conversation again. I was one of the girls. But when I got in the car and looked in the mirror, I didn't recognize the old lady staring back at me. I was not their age at all, but an older, middle aged woman." It made her quite sad and depressed.

That's what I'm talking about. It takes time to adjust to the new you. What helps me get through these sad times is to remind myself that a part of the "young me" is still alive and kicking. My personality hasn't changed; my interests and activities haven't either save for my former career. WHAT IS MOST IMPORTANT TO PASS ON TO MY DAUGHTERS IS

THAT WITH THE SO CALLED AGING PROCESS COMES WISDOM. THAT'S THE GOOD PART. I have gained so much knowledge from all my life experiences. It isn't just the knowing what to do and when to do; it's learning patience, compassion, understanding and love. You can't get all that in the twenties, thirties and forties. It's a process.

I'm getting more and more comfortable with the new me. I have come to accept my body for what it is and I am determined to keep it healthy. So I have to give away all those gorgeous clothes in size 8 and 10—so what? I get to buy new stuff. So I don't wear matching heels and purse, silk scarves and broaches every day. My wardrobe is still stylish yet a lot more casual. I look forward to dressy occasions to sport my lovely accessories from the "old days." So my hair isn't as thick as it used to be. There are products and vitamins out there to help a little. My attitude is getting better each day. Mostly because I am learning to love myself just as I am, and mostly because I enjoy the respect and love of a wonderful man and a great family of four adult children and six grandchildren—so far.

WHAT TO DO WHEN A DOOR CLOSES

Cathy Horvath

I have often heard the phrase, "When one door closes, another opens." Well, my experience with "doors" in my life is a little different. What I have learned through the years is that when your life wants to shut a door and you won't let it, things can get rough. Oh, they may turn out in the end just the way you wanted, but it was a battle all the way to make things happen. When all is said and done, there comes a time when you realize perhaps what you wanted wasn't in your best interest after all. On the other hand, when I have done all I could and turned the rest over to the Universe, things go a whole lot smoother. There have been times in my life when I never dreamed how things would turn out. Here are a couple of examples of what I mean:

When we were first married, we put an offer on a house located right across the street from my grandparents' home. I loved that little four room place and envisioned living out the American dream with husband and children. But it turned out the house was under contract to another buyer and should never have been sold to us until that sale was released. Well, I cried and cried; I prayed and prayed—I wanted that house and no other. The real estate agent showed us others, but I wanted that one and only that one. Well, we finally got the house and spent nine and a half years spending every last dime we had and then some to landscape, build a garage, install storm windows and screens, and several other improvements to make it livable. As time passed we outgrew the small home. Due to some unfortunate circumstances that affected our market, we wound up selling the house for less than what we paid for it and all the improvements we had made. To make matters even worse, we paid the buyers' points according to FHA law, and the realtor's commission. All we had was the little money we could save throughout those years. We wound up living in an apartment for two and a half years to save enough for a down payment on another home.

Another case in point: a friend of mine was extremely unhappy with her current job and prepared for days for an interview for an important new position with a different company in the same industry. We worked on her image, interviewing skills, etc. We knew full well that she possessed all the skills and experience the job required. She prayed, she visualized the scenario where she was offered the position, then she prayed some more because she really wanted that job. To top it off, she had personal recommendations that should have put her at the top of the candidate list. We met for coffee after the interview and to my amazement this calm, level headed, and strong person fell apart at the seams as she related how awful she had performed. What she described wasn't at all like her and neither of us could figure out what happened. All I could think of was that it just wasn't meant to be but that was of little comfort to her. We parted company that evening and for days we kept trying to figure out how she had fumbled so badly when she knew what to say, what to do, sand was perfectly suited to the job.

Fast forward four months: word came out that the division for which she was interviewing was terminated and all employees let go. She would have been out of a job right then and there. The following month a friend recommended her for another position in an even larger, more successful company. She interviewed with confidence this time and nailed the job. She is earning more money than the former position would have offered and is very happy with her new responsibilities. The difference? This time she prayed for guidance, stopped struggling with the outcome, and turned it over to God/ the Universe/or Higher Power. Whatever name you want to call it.

Years ago, I interviewed for a position for which I was highly qualified. I had more experience than the other candidates and was confident I was a shoe in. I never even dreamed otherwise, so it came as a shock when another person was chosen. As I look back, I can't get over how devastated I was.

There was no comparison between us, but as my coworkers pointed out, there are always extenuating circumstances of which I wasn't aware. A year later I took a position with a major real estate company in the Chicago area. As the new Director, I guided the relocation department through new processes and procedures and expanded the client base substantially. Within a year and a half, the division received regional and national recognition for outstanding performance. The very people who were instrumental in not hiring me for that first job I described, stood on a stage in a hotel ballroom with over 750 professionals in attendance, my associates, vice president and myself included. These same people awarded me and my division seven awards for outstanding achievement in the industry. No one had accomplished that before or since! I guess God knew what he was doing in guiding me to the position with a new employer where I would be appreciated, supported and recognized!

A friend said something that has really stuck with me and I think applies to these experiences. Set your goal, envision the outcome, but don't forget when you ask for spiritual guidance to be sure to say something like: "I ask that this job, house, car, etc. be mine or **something better.**" You never know what life has in store for you that could be a whole lot more than what you can dream for yourself.

WHERE'S AN ANGEL WHEN YOU NEED ONE?

This story is an example of the many gifts or bonuses we get from God that come just at the right time:

Patrick C. Blaney, D.D.S.   My wife talked me into going to the Illinois State Fair to enter my daughter Kelly's art project which had won at the County level. I really didn't want to go. It was so far away. It seemed to involve a lot of stress since we didn't have a place to stay, the weather was really hot, and I didn't know where the fair was located, etc.

The trip did not start off well because the car air conditioning broke and the heat was really making me crabby. Then we couldn't get a room for under $225 a night. (This was 18 years ago.) We were late arriving at the fairgrounds. To make matters worse, my wife, Jan, dropped us off at the wrong entrance. That entrance was as far away from where we had to go as an entrance could possibly be. I was just thinking I was going to make Jan suffer for all my stress and suffering when a man pulled up in a golf cart and asked if he could help us. I quickly explained our situation. If we didn't get to the correct location in 10 minutes or less our whole trip was a waste. He told us to hop in and he drove us to where we needed to be. We walked in with minutes to spare and we submitted Kelly's painting. It would have taken us 20 minutes to walk to where we needed to be. Realizing how generous God was to send the "angel" to save us practically made me cry. Kelly ended up with another blue ribbon and Jan and I never got into a fight. Life was good then and still is. God is Great!

WHY WE HAVE TO LEARN LIFE'S LESSONS

I first met the author of this story at a national conference and I was immediately taken with her quiet, gentle demeanor. When my business associates and I gathered together at these meetings, most of the conversations revolved around clients' demands, new procedures, opportunities for revenue, etc. For the most part it was all business. However, this lady always took the time to seek me out and ask how I was doing. Not my department, not my company—me. I was truly impressed with her and have to admit that her personal interest in me set her apart from most of the others. Years later, when I announced my departure from the industry, she sent me the loveliest book. It's called *"This Is My Wish For You."* It remains on my nightstand to this day and whenever I reminisce about those days, the book reminds me of one very special, lovely friend. Here's her contribution to this book:

"I heard a story about a man whose Father died when he was very young, around five or six. This young lad had a wonderful childhood and grew into an amazing business man, husband and father. As magnificent as his life was there was always a sadness within him because of the loss of his father at such a young age.

Years later his son passed away, leaving behind a wife and several small children. Again, though it was so difficult for this loving Father, he continued to move forward with his usual optimism. For financial reasons, the daughter-in-law and small children ended up moving in with the grandparents which brought them great joy. He felt years younger and loved the opportunity to participate more in their lives.

One of his grandsons was having such a difficult time with the death of his father. The Grandfather sat with him one evening and shared with him the story of his youth. He related that at about the same age he had lost his father also and it was so difficult for him. Throughout his life he wondered why this had happened to him. He still wonders; there really is no satisfactory answer for questions like this. Yet he knew since he had already walked the path his grandson was walking, he would be able to help him every step of the way."

Jeanne Johnson is a unique and multi-faceted woman. For years she struggled with an illness that all but controlled her life. Determined to break free of this existence and raise her four children, she began a journey of self healing. When she emerged from this experience, she had been gifted with the ability to heal with her hands. Today she is a spiritual healer and a practitioner of various healing modalities. She is a dear and very special friend.

Jeanne Johnson
(aka Little Dove)

"My grandparents and indeed most of my extended family were subsistence farmers. Each member of the extended family raised a different animal. My grandfather raised cows. One uncle raised dairy cattle, another pigs. Everyone raised chickens and had at least one milking cow. Everyone had a garden and a fruit orchard. Vegetables and fruits were canned and stored in root cellars for eating in the winter. Wild berries were collected and baked into pies and cooked into jams. Acres of hay were grown to feed the live-stock. Haying was a community activity done in late summer every year. Men folk gathered and harvested fields in turn. Women folk cooked big meals. Fried chicken, mashed potatoes, fresh tomatoes, corn on the cob, bread with cow's butter, cow's milk and homemade pies. The men came in at lunch and feasted then headed back to the field. Cow's milk and cow's butter (to distinguish the fresh raw variety from the watery flat tasting stuff that came from the grocery store) were part of the daily meals. Cow's milk came straight from the cow. Grandpa walked up to the barn in the early morning with the milking bucket in hand. The barn cats waited by the back door, mewing. The cats swirled around his feet and trotted beside him up the path to the barnyard. The cow just stood there, nothing holding it, just swishing the flies away with her tail. Grandpa grabbed the teats and squeezed and pulled on them and the milk squirted out hitting the bottom of the metal bucket making a flat squir-ting- squir-ting- squir- ting. The cats sat in a semicircle just to the side of Grandpa and every once in a while he angled the teat toward them and squirted milk in the direction of their open mouths.

They caught a good bit of it. When he was done he carried the bucket back to the house. By the time he got there the cream was sitting on top of the milk. Grandma would skim most of it off, but not all and put the milk in a pitcher and refrigerate it. Usually the calves came from the cows that grandpa owned, but occasionally he bought a calf and hand raise it. The calf started out drinking milk out of a bucket just like the milking bucket but with a rubber teat on one side toward the bottom. The calf had foamy milk gushing out the side of its mouth as he hungrily sucked on the rubber teat.

Occasionally Grandpa sold a cow for cash at the livestock auction held once a week in town. I rode along in the bed of his old pick-up and he would head to the auction barn. Girls didn't go there. I went to the town library, which was housed in the front room of some lady's house and then to the general store for a soda pop or ice cream bar. Men sat outside the store and chewed tobacco, spitting brown spittle, talking and laughing with tobacco stained teeth. One week each summer there was Vacation Bible School. Someone came around each morning in their pick-up truck and children climbed in and sat down. We were instructed to sit but sometimes we stood right behind the cab with the wind blowing against our faces. We were delivered to the Valley Center Baptist Church and spent the day learning Bible verses, songs and making crafts with sewing spindles, macaroni noodles and gold or silver spray paint. A snack of Kool-Aid and stale cookies, and another ride in the truck. The truck ride was worth having to endure the rest.

My grandparents were Zen Masters who had never heard of Zen. Their lives were an active meditation. They were conscious in the taking of life to have sustenance for their own lives and thankful for the opportunity to live. Their food was clean, the air was clean, the water from their well was clean and their thoughts were clean. I never heard either of them ever say a discouraging word about another human being.

My grandmother taught me about spirituality of another sort. She didn't preach or teach with words. Her faith was a walk with God. I saw her take some time each day to sit and commune with the Bible. She had a relationship with those pages that spoke volumes about how to be in Spirit. I never saw her on her knees, never witnessed a pious moment. What I did witness was a light in her eyes that few people have. I saw a peace and happiness in her countenance. I felt loved and accepted by her in every way.

I strive to be like my grandparents in spiritual living. I have learned that the spiritual element of Love is the only ingredient, tool, weapon, prescription that always produces a good outcome. Love is as readily available, abundant and necessary to good life as the air we breathe. The spiritual element of Love is not an emotion; it is a state of being. Nourishment of our body, mind, emotions and spirit is a personal responsibility.

It is true that the taste of animals raised by hand is different from the mass produced flesh we consume. The taste of fruits and vegetables home grown is better than those grown in mass plantings or greenhouses. I think it has to do with whether or not our food has been touched with Love. The blessing of food for me has become the spiritual healing of the food and all those who have touched it along the way. The food often has to have its energy transmuted to reduce the amount of toxins that reside in it from chemicals that have been knowingly added and from those that we unconsciously add with our thoughts and attitudes.

People say that my recipes do not taste the same when they cook them. I tell them that I always add a secret ingredient. "What secret ingredient? What is it?" "The Secret is Love."

ABOUT CATHY HORVATH

A native of Chicago, Cathy along with her husband, Ray, moved to the Atlanta area when she took a job with a new employer. Prior to that, she was Vice President of Corporate Relocation, where she directed one of the largest real estate divisions that serviced incoming and outbound transferees. She enjoyed national visibility as a recipient of numerous awards, (exceeding industry records). She was well known as a speaker locally, regionally and nationally. She facilitated training workshops for real estate agents and relocation professionals alike, and was featured in Chicago newspapers and Relocation Industry magazines as an outstanding and accomplished female.

When her corporate days ended, she took a position as Events Manager for The Mansell House & Gardens in Alpharetta, GA. Scheduling weddings, parties and corporate events was the most enjoyable job she ever held. She supervised the redecorating of the one hundred year old home originally owned by Mr. & Mrs. Robert Mansell. Not one to accept the status quo, she co-founded the Wedding Alliance of North Georgia. As a member of the board, Cathy participated in the planning and execution of several Special Events and Bridal Expos. Two years later, she left to pursue her dream. *RECIPES FOR LIFE: Food for the Body and Nourishment for the Soul* took three years to complete. It is a compilation of contributions from family, friends and former business associates from all over this country and from nine others as well.

She and her husband Ray have four grown children, two men and two women, and six grandchildren ranging in age from ten to 26. As much as she enjoyed her life in the corporate world, her family and this book are her passion.

Contact Cathy for speaking engagements at
www.RecipesforLifeBodyandSoul.com
RecipesforLifeBodyandSoul@gmail.com

www.RecipesforLifeBodyandSoul.com